THE TRUTH ABOUT MAN

THIRD EDITION

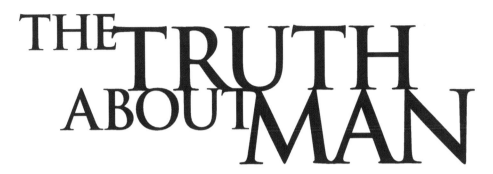

THE TRUTH ABOUT MAN

A BIBLICAL STUDY OF THE DOCTRINE OF MAN

PAUL DAVID WASHER

WWW.HEARTCRYMISSIONARY.COM

THE TRUTH ABOUT MAN

THE TRUTH ABOUT MAN
Copyright © 2004 by Paul David Washer of HeartCry Missionary Society.
Published by HeartCry Missionary Society.

PUBLICATION HISTORY:
 1st Edition printed in 2007.
 2nd Edition, revised and reformatted, published in 2009 by Granted Ministries Press.
 3rd Edition, HeartCry Missionary Society in 2011.

Cover design and graphics by Jonathan Green.

For information or additional copies of *The Truth about Man* and other
resources write:

HEARTCRY MISSIONARY SOCIETY
P.O. Box 2309
Radford, VA 24068 USA
www.heartcrymissionary.com
info@heartcrymissionary.com
540-707-1005

All Scripture quotations taken from the New American Standard Bible®,
Copyright © 1960, 1962, 1963, 1968, 1971, 1972, 1973, 1975, 1977, 1995
by The Lockman Foundation. Used by permission.

ISBN: 1466316241   ISBN 13: 978-1466316249

TABLE OF CONTENTS

ACKNOWLEDGMENTS

I would like to thank my wife Charo who is growing to be "strong in the Lord," and my three children Ian, Evan, and Rowan who are able to pull me away from my work with a glance. I would also like to thank the staff at HeartCry who encouraged me to publish this work, and Pastor Charles Leiter of Kirksville, Missouri, whose insights were invaluable.

INTRODUCTION

METHOD OF STUDY

The great goal of this study is for the student to have an encounter with God through His Word. Founded upon the conviction that the Scriptures are the inspired and infallible Word of God, this study has been designed in such a way that it is literally impossible for the student to advance without an open Bible before him or her. Our goal is to obey the exhortation of the apostle Paul in II Timothy 2:15:

"Be diligent to present yourself approved to God as a workman who does not need to be ashamed, accurately handling the word of truth."

Each lesson deals with a specific aspect of the doctrine of man. The student will complete each lesson by answering the questions according to the Scriptures given. The student is encouraged to meditate upon each text and write his or her thoughts. The benefit reaped from this study will depend upon the student's investment. If the student answers the questions by thoughtlessly copying the text and without seeking to understand its meaning, very little will be gained.

The student will find that this is primarily a Biblical study and does not contain much in the way of colorful illustrations or quaint stories, nor even a great amount of theological commentary. It was our desire to provide a work that only pointed the way to the Scriptures and allowed the Scriptures to speak for themselves.

This book may be used by an individual, small group, or Sunday school class. It is highly recommended that the student complete each chapter on his or her own before meeting for discussion and questions with the group or discipleship leader.

EXHORTATION TO THE STUDENT

Through the use of this book the student is encouraged to study biblical doctrine and discover its exalted place in the Christian life. The true Christian cannot bear or even survive a divorce between the emotions and the intellect, or between devotion to God and the truth of God. According to the Scriptures, neither our emotions nor our experiences provide an adequate foundation for the Christian life. Only the truths of Scripture, understood with the mind and communicated through doctrine, can provide that sure foundation upon which we should establish our beliefs and behavior as well as determine the validity of our emotions and experiences. *The mind is not the enemy of the heart, and doctrine is not an obstacle to devotion.* The two are indispensable and should be inseparable. The Scriptures command us to love the Lord our God with all our heart, with all our soul, and with all our mind (Matthew 22:37), and to worship God in both spirit and in truth (John 4:24).

The study of doctrine is both an intellectual and devotional discipline. It is a passionate search for God that should always lead the student to greater personal transformation, obedience, and heartfelt worship. Therefore, the student should be on guard against the great error of seeking only impersonal knowledge and not the person of God. Neither mindless devotion nor mere intellectual pursuit is profitable, for in either case God is lost.

THE NEW AMERICAN STANDARD VERSION

While there are many good English translations of the Bible, this study was developed for use with the New American Standard Version. This version is not absolutely required to complete the study, but there may be times when the student will notice a minor difference if they use a different translation (especially if they are using a less accurate, non-literal translation). This translation of Scripture was chosen for the following reasons: (1) the unwavering conviction of the translators that the Bible is the infallible Word of God, and (2) its faithfulness to the original languages.

"... we shall never have an adequate conception of the greatness of this salvation unless we realize something at any rate of what we were before this mighty power took hold of us, unless we realize what we would still be if God had not intervened in our lives and had rescued us. In other words, we must realize the depth of sin, what sin really means, and what it has done to the human race."

– DR. MARTYN LLOYD-JONES –
(EPHESIANS, VOLUME TWO, P. 14)

"Without a knowledge of our unfaithfulness and rebellion we will never come to know God as the God of truth and grace. Without a knowledge of our pride we will never know Him in His greatness. Nor will we come to Him for the healing we need. When we are sick physically and know that we are sick, we seek out a doctor and follow his prescription for a cure. But if we did not know we were sick, we would not seek help and might well perish from the illness. It is the same spiritually. If we think we are well, we will never accept God's cure; we think we do not need it. Instead, if by God's grace we become aware of our sickness—actually, of something worse than sickness, of spiritual death so far as any meaningful response to God is concerned—then we have a basis for understanding the meaning of Christ's work on our behalf, and can embrace Him as Savior and be transformed by Him."

– JAMES MONTGOMERY BOYCE –
(FOUNDATIONS OF THE CHRISTIAN FAITH, P. 198)

"There is no better way of testing our understanding of the Christian doctrine of salvation than to examine our understanding of the true nature of sin."

– DR. MARTYN LLOYD JONES –
(ROMANS, 7:1-8:4, P. 119)

"THEN GOD SAID, 'LET US MAKE MAN IN OUR IMAGE, ACCORDING TO OUR LIKENESS; AND LET THEM RULE OVER THE FISH OF THE SEA AND OVER THE BIRDS OF THE SKY AND OVER THE CATTLE AND OVER ALL THE EARTH, AND OVER EVERY CREEPING THING THAT CREEPS ON THE EARTH.'"

– GENESIS 1:26 –

"COME, LET US WORSHIP AND BOW DOWN, LET US KNEEL BEFORE THE LORD OUR MAKER."

– PSALM 95:6 –

THE CREATION OF MAN

The Scriptures teach us that man is not an accident or the result of some mindless process, but the creative work of the eternal God. After God had created all other creatures, He formed the first man Adam from the dust of the ground, breathed the breath of life into his nostrils, and he became a living being. From Adam, God then formed the woman Eve to be both a companion and helper to Adam. They were commanded to multiply and fill the earth which had been placed under their dominion. All mankind finds its common ancestry in this union of Adam and Eve.

Unique among all other creatures, only man and woman were created in the *imago dei* [Latin: *imago*, image + *dei*, of God] and granted the privilege of living in personal and unbroken fellowship with Him. The Scripture is also clear that they were created *by* God and *for* God and find meaning for their existence only in loving Him, glorifying Him, and doing His will.

These truths are of great importance for us in that they define who we are and the purpose for which we were made. We are not the authors of our own existence, but we were brought into existence by the gracious will and power of God. We do not belong to ourselves, but to God who made us for His own purposes and good pleasure. To seek to separate from God in any way is to sever ourselves from life. To live independently of His person and will is to deny the purpose for which we were made.

1. In the second chapter of Genesis is found the Scripture's account of the creation of man. Based on **Genesis 2:7**, summarize this account. What does it communicate to us about the origin of man and his relationship to God?

2. Also in the second chapter of Genesis is the Scripture's account of the creation of the first woman. Based on **Genesis 2:21-23**, summarize the biblical account of woman's creation. What does it communicate to us about her origin and relationship to God?

3. Having established the truth about man—that he is the creative work of God— we must now consider his uniqueness among the rest of creation. According to the following phrases from **Genesis 1:26-28**, how is man unique from the rest of creation?

   a. *"Let us make man..."*

Note: God does not say, "Let there be," as with the rest of creation (1:3, 6, 14), but "Let us make." This communicates the idea of greater personal relationship. The phrase "Let us..." has been interpreted several ways: (1) Some say it is a plural of majesty. They assert that it was common in the ancient world for royalty to speak as a plurality. One main problem with this view is that the Hebrew plural of majesty is used only with nouns—not with pronouns like "us." (2) Some say that God is speaking to angels. If true, this would imply that angels are also made in God's image, something that is possible, but not explicitly stated anywhere in Scripture. Also, in v. 27, there is a singular Creator and not many: "God created" … "He created" … "He created." This could not be if the 'us' referred to God and angels. Furthermore, in the final judgment, human believers are the judges of angels (I Corinthians 6:3), and it would be very odd for creatures to be judging their creators. (3) Some say it is a reference to the persons of the Trinity taking counsel with one another. This last interpretation is the most likely, as we have clear texts in Scripture demonstrating that the creation does indeed involve the Father, the Spirit (Genesis 1:2) and the Son (John 1:1-3; Colossians 1:16). This explains the plural "Let us..." in v. 26. It also explains why there appears to be only one Creator in v. 27: God is one divine Being who nonetheless exists as three divine Persons.

b. *"... in our image..."*

_____

_____

_____

_____

_____

Note: God did not say, "after their kind," as with the rest of creation (Genesis 1:11-12, 21, 24-25), but "in our image." Humanity is unique among creation in that it alone is said to bear the *imago dei*. The image of God may refer to the following:

Personality: Adam and Eve were personal and self-conscious creatures. They were not mere animals driven by instinct or machines programmed to respond to certain stimuli.

Spirituality: The Scriptures declare that "God is Spirit" (John 4:24), and so it is reasonable to expect to find this same attribute in man who was created in God's image. Adam and Eve were more than animated clay; they were spiritual, endowed with a genuine capacity to know God, fellowship with God, and respond to God in obedience, adoration, and thanksgiving.

Knowledge: In Colossians 3:10, the Scriptures describe one aspect of the image of God as having a true knowledge of God. This does not mean that Adam and Eve knew all that can be known about God—a finite creature can never fully comprehend an infinite God (Psalm 145:3). Rather, it means that the knowledge they did possess was pure or unalloyed.

Self-Determination or *Will*: Adam and Eve were created with a will; they possessed the power of self-determination, and they were granted the freedom to choose.

Immortality: Although Adam and Eve were created and therefore had a beginning, and although every moment of their very existence depended upon the kindness of their Creator, they were endowed with an immortal soul—once created, it would never cease to exist. The immortality of the soul should lead all men to consider carefully the awesome responsibility of self-determination. Since the soul is eternal, the choices we make will bear eternal consequences from which there may be no escape.

c. *"... let them rule..."*

_____

_____

_____

_____

Note: Man and woman were given the privilege and responsibility of ruling over all creation as vice-regents of God. Their rule was not to be independent of God's, but in perfect conformity to His will. Therefore, they were to exercise their rule with lovingkindness for the benefit and care of a good creation and for the glory of God.

4. In Genesis 1:26-28, we learned that man is unique among the rest of creation in that he alone was created in the image of God. In the following Scriptures, we will discover that, although man is unique, he shares a common purpose with the rest of creation: he was not made for himself, but for the glory and good pleasure of God. What do the following Scriptures teach us about this truth?

Psalm 104:31

_____

_____

_____

_____

Romans 11:36

_____

_____

_____

_____

Colossians 1:16

_____

_____

5. The Scriptures teach that man and woman were created by God and for God, and find meaning for their existence only in loving Him, glorifying Him, and doing His will. We are not the authors of our own existence, but we were brought into existence by the gracious will and power of God. We do not belong to ourselves, but to God who made us for His own purposes and good pleasure. In light of these great truths, how should mankind respond?

a. *Fear and Awe:* **Psalm 33:6-9**

b. *Worship:* **Psalm 95:6**

c. *Love:* **Mark 12:28-30**

d. *Service:* **Psalm 100:1-3**

e. *Glory and Honor:* ***I Corinthians 10:31***

"Behold, I have found only this, that God made men upright, but they have sought out many devices."

– Ecclesiastes 7:29 –

THE FALL OF ADAM

In accordance with His own purpose and good pleasure, God created Adam and Eve and commanded them not to eat of the tree of knowledge of good and evil. Obedience to the command would lead to a continued life, both of joyful fellowship with God and of dominion over creation. Disobedience to the command would lead to spiritual and physical death and all the accompanying maladies.

Adam and Eve were tempted and disobeyed the command. Because of their disobedience, their fellowship with God was broken and they fell from their original state of righteousness and holiness. These devastating consequences of Adam's disobedience were not limited to him, but resulted in the fall of the entire human race. Although the Scriptures do not remove all mystery surrounding this great truth, they affirm that the sin and guilt of Adam has been *imputed,* or credited, to all his descendants, and that all men without exception are now born bearing Adam's fallen nature and exhibiting Adam's hostility toward God.

These points will be discussed in the next several lessons, beginning with the Fall of Adam.

THE FALL OF ADAM

After God created Adam in His image, He gave him a simple command: "From the tree of the knowledge of good and evil you shall not eat." A warning followed this prohibition: "In the day that you eat from it you will surely die" (Genesis 2:17). Adam's obedience to God would lead to a continued or possibly even greater state of blessedness. His disobedience would lead to death.

1. In **Genesis 2:16-17** are found the commandment and warning given to Adam. Read the text until you are familiar with its contents and then answer the following questions:

   a. *According to verse 16, what privilege did God give to Adam? How does this privilege prove that God cared about Adam and did not disregard his needs?*

   _____

   _____

   _____

   _____

   _____

   b. *According to verse 17, what prohibition was placed upon Adam? What was Adam commanded not to do?*

   _____

   _____

   _____

   _____

   c. *According to verse 17, what would be the penalty for disobeying God's command?*

   _____

   _____

   _____

   _____

2. In **Genesis 3:1-6** is found the biblical account of how Adam and Eve were tempted to disobey God's command. Read the text until you are familiar with its contents and then answer the following questions:

   a. *In verse 1, the Scriptures declare that a literal serpent tempted Eve. According to* **Revelation 12:9** *and* **20:2**, *who was the one working in and through the serpent?*

   _____

   _____

   _____

b. *According to verse 4-5, what promise did Satan make to Eve?*

c. *According to verse 6, how did Eve and her husband Adam respond to Satan's temptation through the serpent?*

3. **Genesis 3:7-10** records the immediate results of Adam and Eve's disobedience. Read the text several times until you are familiar with its contents and then write your thoughts. What were the results of their disobedience?

   a. *Verse 7*

   b. *Verses 8-10*

> **Note:** (a) With one act of disobedience, Adam and Eve fell from their original state of righteousness into moral corruption. Their hearts and minds were no longer pure, but became defiled and shameful. The coverings they made from fig leaves were a feeble attempt to hide their shame, sin, and corruption. (b) Sin always results in fear and separation from God. Sinful man runs from God's holy presence and fears His righteous judgment.

4. Having considered the immediate results of Adam's disobedience, we will now consider the divine judgments that fell upon the serpent, Eve, and Adam. Read **Genesis 3:14-24** and then describe these judgments that have affected us all:

a. *The Divine Judgment upon the Serpent (vs. 14-15):*

b. *The Divine Judgment upon the Woman (v. 16):*

> **Note:** The phrase, "Your desire will be for your husband," may describe one of the following: (1) The woman's relationship with her husband would be marked by longing and lack of fulfillment. (2) The woman who sought independence from God would now have an inordinate desire or craving for man. (3) The relationship between man and woman would be marked by conflict; the woman would "desire" to dominate her husband, and her husband would exert his "rule" over her. The third interpretation seems especially likely in light of the similar wording in Genesis 4:7: "And if you do not do well, sin is crouching at the door; *and its desire is for you, but you must master it."*

c. *The Divine Judgment upon the Man (vs. 17-19):*

5. In the divine judgment upon the serpent in **Genesis 3:14-15** is found one of the greatest promises of salvation in the entire Bible (v. 15). It has been called the *protevangelium* [Latin: *proto*, first + *evangelium*, gospel]. Write your comments on this text.

_____

_____

_____

_____

Note: Jesus Christ is the eventual "seed" or offspring of the woman. On the cross, Satan bruised Christ's heel (*i.e.* Christ was wounded, but not mortally; He rose from the dead). Through that same cross, Christ bruised Satan on the head (*i.e.* Satan was mortally wounded; he has been forever defeated).

IMPORTANT QUESTIONS ABOUT THE FALL

The Scriptural account of the fall provides the only adequate explanation of man's present fallen state and the evil that surrounds us. It is also upon this dark background that the bright glories of God's mercy and grace appear. Only to the degree that we understand the tragedy of Adam and his condemnation can we comprehend something of the glories of Christ and His Gospel.

In our study of the fall, we are faced with some of the most important and complex theological questions in all of Scripture: the origin of evil, the nature of human freedom, the sovereignty of God, and His eternal purpose. *Although what we know about these issues will always be mingled with a certain degree of mystery, it is necessary that we endeavor to know what we can.* We will address the following questions below:

How could Adam fall?
Did God ordain the fall?
What is God's eternal purpose in the fall?

HOW COULD ADAM FALL?

The Scriptures affirm that the fall was not due to any fault in the Creator. All God's works are perfect (Deuteronomy 32:4), He cannot be tempted by sin (James 1:13), nor does He tempt others with sin (James 1:13). The blame for the fall rests squarely upon the shoulders of Adam. As Ecclesiastes 7:29 declares, "Behold, I have found only this, that God made men *upright*, but they have sought out many devices."

This truth presents one of the greatest theological problems in all the Scriptures: how is it possible that a creature created in the image of God came to choose evil and sin? Adam and Eve had a true inclination toward good, and there was nothing corrupt or evil in them to which temptation might appeal. How such righteous beings could choose evil over good, and choose the words of a serpent over the commands of their Creator, is beyond human comprehension.

There have been numerous attempts throughout history to explain the fall of Adam, but none of them is without its limitations. We must therefore be content with the simple truth of Scripture that although God made man righteous and holy, he was *finite* and *mutable* (*i.e.* subject to change) and capable of making a choice contrary to the will of God.

DID GOD ORDAIN THE FALL?

The word *ordain* means to *put in order, arrange,* or *appoint.* To ask if God ordained the fall is to ask if He put it in order, arranged it, or appointed that it occur. Other words that carry similar meaning are: "decree," "predetermine," and "predestine." Did God determine beforehand or decree that the fall should occur? The answer to this question is "yes," but we must be very careful that we understand what this *does* and *does not* mean.

God's ordaining of the fall *does not* mean that He forced Satan to tempt our first parents, or that He coerced them to disregard His command. What God's creatures did, they did willingly. God is holy, just, and good. He does not sin, cannot be tempted by sin, and He does not tempt anyone to sin.

God's ordaining of the fall *does* mean that it was certain to happen. It was God's will that Adam be tested, and it was God's will to let Adam both stand and fall alone without the divine aid which could have kept him from falling. God could have hindered Satan from laying the temptation before Eve, or in the face of such temptation

He could have given Adam special sustaining grace to enable him to triumph over it. From the testimony of the Scriptures, we understand that He did not.

God's ordaining of the fall also means that it was a part of His eternal plan. Before the foundation of the world, before the creation of Adam and Eve and the serpent that tempted them, before the existence of any garden or tree, God ordained the fall for His glory and the greater good of His creation. He did not merely permit our first parents to be tempted and then wait to react to whatever choice they made. He did not merely look through the corridors of time and see the fall. Rather, the fall was a part of God's eternal plan and He predetermined or predestined that it should and would happen.

At this point a very important question arises:

"Is God the author of sin?"

This question can and should be answered with a strong negative. God is not the author of sin, nor does He coerce men to sin against Him. Although He predetermined that the fall *should* and *would* happen, He also predetermined that it should happen through the willing actions of Satan, Adam, and Eve. Although our finite minds cannot fully comprehend how God can be absolutely sovereign over every event of history and over every individual act without destroying individual freedom, the Scriptures abound with examples that demonstrate this to be true. Joseph was sold into slavery as a result of the willful sin of his brothers, and yet when the final story was told, Joseph declared, "As for you, *you meant* evil against me, but *God meant* it for good in order to bring about this present result, to preserve many people alive" (Genesis 50:20). The Son of God was crucified as a result of man's willful sin and hostility toward God, and yet God had ordained or predetermined the death of Christ before the foundation of the world. In the Scriptures we read:

"… this Man, delivered over by the predetermined plan and foreknowledge of God, you nailed to a cross by the hands of godless men and put Him to death."
-Acts 2:23

"For truly in this city there were gathered together against Your holy servant Jesus, whom You anointed, both Herod and Pontius Pilate, along with the Gentiles and the peoples of Israel, to do whatever Your hand and Your purpose predestined to occur."
-Acts 4:27-28

From the Scriptures, we see that God does ordain or predetermine an event to occur and yet brings it to pass through the willful sin of men. He does this without being the author of their sin or coercing them to do that which is against their will. Godless men willfully nailed Jesus Christ to the cross and were responsible for their actions, but the entire event was according to the predetermined plan of God. The fall of Satan, and the later fall of the human race through Adam and Eve, were the results of their own sin for which they alone were responsible, and yet the events came to pass according to the ordained, predetermined, predestined plan of God. God has decreed a great eternal purpose for His creation and has ordained every event of history by which that purpose is being fulfilled. Nothing, not even the fall of man or the death of God's Son, occurs apart from the sovereign decree of God.

> 'Oh, the depth of the riches both of the wisdom and knowledge of God! How unsearchable are His judgments and unfathomable His ways! For "who has known the mind of the Lord, or who became His counselor?" Or "who has first given to Him that it might be paid back to Him again?" **For from Him and through Him and to Him are all things.** To Him be the glory forever. Amen.'
> -Romans 11:33-36

> "… In Him also we have obtained an inheritance, having been predestined according to His purpose **who works all things after the counsel of His will**.…"
> -Ephesians 1:10-11

WHAT IS GOD'S ETERNAL PURPOSE IN THE FALL?

Having demonstrated that the fall was the result of the creature's willful disobedience and yet also according to the eternal purpose of God, it is now necessary that we endeavor to know that eternal purpose. In light of the evil and suffering that has resulted from the fall, it may seem difficult to accept that there can be any good purpose in it. Nevertheless, God's Word assures us that there is such a purpose.

We know from the Scriptures that the creation of the universe, the fall of man, the nation of Israel, the cross of Christ, the Church, and the judgment of the nations have *one great and final purpose*. It is that the fullness of God's attributes be revealed to His creation and that all creation know Him, glorify Him, and fully enjoy Him as God.

The Full Revelation of God's Attributes

God created the universe to be a theater upon which He might display the infinite glory and worth of His being and attributes, that He might be fully known, worshipped, and enjoyed by His creation. It has been said by many that the fall of man is the pitch-black sky upon which the stars of God's attributes shine with the greatest intensity of glory. It is only through the fall and the advent of evil that the fullness of God's character may truly be known.

When the Christian worships God, what are the attributes that seem most dear to him? Are they not God's mercy, grace, and unconditional love? Are these not the divine attributes most exalted in all the great hymns of the Church? Yet how could these attributes be known except through the fall of man? Unconditional love can only be manifest upon men who do not meet the conditions. Mercy can only be poured forth from the throne of God upon men who deserve condemnation. Grace can only be granted to men who have done nothing to earn it. Our fallenness is our doing, for which we are obliged to take full responsibility. Yet it is through the dark theater of our fallenness that the grace and mercy of God takes center stage and shine forth upon an audience of both men and angels. It is in the salvation of fallen man that the wisdom, grace, and mercy of God are revealed, not only to man but also to every created being in heaven, earth, and hell.

> *But God, being rich in mercy, because of His great love with which He loved us, even when we were dead in our transgressions, made us alive together with Christ (by grace you have been saved), and raised us up with Him, and seated us with Him in the heavenly places in Christ Jesus, so that in the ages to come He might show the surpassing riches of His grace in kindness toward us in Christ Jesus.*
> *-Ephesians 2:4-7*

> *To me, the very least of all saints, this grace was given, to preach to the Gentiles the unfathomable riches of Christ, and to bring to light what is the administration of the mystery which for ages has been hidden in God who created all things; so that the manifold wisdom of God might now be made known through the church to the rulers and the authorities in the heavenly places.*
> *-Ephesians 3:8-10*

The Full Revelation of the Glories of Christ

The greatest work of God is the death and resurrection of the Son of God for the salvation of God's people. However, if man had not fallen there would have been no Calvary and no Savior. The very thing that most explains God (John 1:18), draws us to Him (John 12:32), and causes us to love Him (I John 4:10, 19) would be gone.

What would take its place? What other means could have been used to demonstrate the immeasurable mercies of God? Christ crucified is the great theme of every worthy Christian hymn, sermon, conversation, and thought. Without the fall, redemption would be unknown to us. We would be like the angels, longing to look upon something that we would never and could never experience (I Peter 1:12).

It is wrong, and near blasphemy, to even hint that the cross of Christ was a mere Plan "B" that was employed only because of Adam's wrong choice in the garden. The cross is the main event to which every other work of God's providence points. All things stand in its shadow. In one sense, the cross was necessary because of the fall, but in another sense, the fall was necessary so that the glories of God in the cross of Christ might be made fully known.

The Full Revelation of the Creature's Dependence

One of the most awe-inspiring and humbling truths about God is that He is absolutely free from any need or dependence (Acts 17:24-25). His existence, the fulfillment of His will, and His happiness or good pleasure do not depend upon anyone or anything outside of Himself. He is the only being who is truly self-existent, self-sustaining, self-sufficient, independent, and free. All other beings derive their life and blessedness from God, but God finds all that is necessary for His own existence and perfect happiness in Himself (Psalm 16:11; Psalm 36:9).

The existence of the universe requires not only the initial act of creation but also the continued power of God to sustain it (Hebrews 1:3). If He were to withdraw His power for even one moment, all would turn to chaos and destruction. This same truth may be applied to the character of moral beings, whether angels or men. Adam in paradise and Satan in heaven, although created righteous and holy, could not stand apart from the sustaining grace of an Almighty God. How much less are we able to stand and how much more quickly would we fall apart from the same sustaining grace? The fall, therefore, provides the greatest example of our constant need for God. If we cannot continue our existence beyond our next breath except for God's preservation, how much less are we able to maintain any semblance of righteousness before Him apart from His grace (John 15:4-5; Philippians 2:12-13)?

"Therefore, just as through one man sin entered into the world, and death through sin, and so death spread to all men, because all sinned..."

– Romans 5:12 –

THE FALL OF MANKIND

The Scriptures which we will study in this section affirm three very important truths about the fall of Adam and its devastating effects upon the entire human race. Apart from these truths, it is *impossible* to account for mankind's moral corruption and the universal presence of evil in a world created good. These three truths are:

1. *God made Adam to be the representative or head of the entire human race.* As head, Adam acted on behalf of all mankind, and the consequences of his actions affect us all.

2. *God "imputed" Adam's sin to all men.* The words "impute" and "imputation" come from the Latin verb *imputare* which means, "to consider, reckon, attribute, or charge to one's account." With regard to the fall, it means that God reckons or charges the sin of Adam to every man's account. From their birth all men are regarded and treated as sinners on account of Adam's sin. All men bear the guilt of Adam's sin and its penalty. (This idea is traditionally known as the doctrine of *original sin*.)

3. *God turned all men over to moral corruption.* The consequence and penalty of Adam's sin was not only death, but also moral corruption. This means that every one of Adam's descendants is born wholly inclined to evil and at enmity with God. Adam fell from his original state of righteousness and became a morally corrupt creature. Since all men bear the guilt of Adam's sin, they also bear the penalty: death and moral corruption. Without the saving grace of God, a man will continue in this morally corrupt state forever.

AN UNDENIABLE TRUTH, AN UNEXPLAINABLE MYSTERY

The fall of mankind in the fall of Adam will always be shrouded in mystery. On the one hand, it is one of the greatest and most essential doctrines in Christianity, it is clearly asserted in Scripture to be true, and it provides the *only* adequate explanation for the universal moral corruption of mankind. At the same time, however, the very Scripture that affirms the doctrine offers little explanation as to how such things can be so, and offers no defense against the frequent accusations that such things are unjust or unfair. How can it be just for God to impute the sin and guilt of Adam to all of mankind? The following points are worthy of consideration:

1. *The truthfulness of a doctrine is not validated by our ability to comprehend it or reconcile it to our understanding, nor is our inability grounds for rejecting it.* If this were the case, there would be no such thing as Christian doctrine, for there is no revealed truth that does not contain some element of mystery. In Deuteronomy 29:29, the Scriptures declare, "The secret things belong to the Lord our God, but the things revealed belong to us and to our sons forever, that we may observe all the words of this law." It is the great promise of Scripture that the truth we believe and yet do not fully understand will one day be made known to us, and the shadow of uncertainty and doubt that yet remains will disappear in the light of God's full revelation. The apostle Paul writes, "For now we see in a mirror dimly, but then face to face; now I know in part, but then I will know fully just as I also have been fully known" (I Corinthians 13:12).

2. *Throughout Scripture, God has so proved His perfect justice in His dealings with man that any and every accusation to the contrary is met with a stern rebuke.* "… God is greater than man. Why do you complain against Him that He does not give an account of all His doings?" (Job 33:12b-13). "On the contrary, who are you, O man, who answers back to God?" (Romans 9:20). If God has made Adam to be the head of the race and imputed his sin to the whole of mankind, it is both just and fair. God has the divine right to purpose and to work according to His own good pleasure. Moreover, God has never acted in any way that would give His creatures a just cause of complaint against Him.

3. *It was a great demonstration of grace that God would allow one man to be tested on behalf of all other men.* Adam was the fittest man of the entire human race and lived in a place untainted by the sin and corruption which now prevails. God chose the greatest and noblest among us to stand in our place.

4. *All the evidence of Scripture, human history, and the inner witness of conscience points to the certainty that any one of Adam's race would have done no better than Adam himself.*

5. *All of Adam's race, as soon as they are able, **willingly** participate in Adam's rebellion against God and so prove that God justly condemns them.*

6. *If it is wrong or unjust for God to condemn the whole human race through the fall of the one man Adam, then it is just as wrong for God to save His people (i.e. the redeemed) through the obedience of the one man Jesus Christ.* If God cannot rightly *impute* Adam's sin to mankind, then He cannot rightly *impute* mankind's sin to Christ to enable Him to die for us, or *impute* Christ's righteousness to those who believe. In that case, all men would stand entirely on their own, without a savior, and therefore all would be damned.

ALL MEN ARE BORN IN SIN

The declaration that "all men are born in sin" means that God has imputed the sin and guilt of Adam to *every one* of his descendants. All men from birth are regarded and treated as sinners on account of Adam's sin. It is important to note that this is not some 'theological theory' or 'philosophical construction,' but it is the clear teaching of the Scriptures and is demonstrated constantly in everyday life.

In **Romans 5:12-19** is found the most important discourse in all of Scripture regarding the fall of Adam and the imputation of his sin to the entire human race. Read the passage until you are familiar with its contents and then explain the meaning of each of the following declarations:

1. *"Therefore, just as through one man sin entered into the world, and death through sin..." (v. 12):*

Note: "… *through one man sin entered into the world…*": The Scriptures affirm that God created all things "very good" (Genesis 1:31). The biblical explanation for the presence of sin in God's good world is that it entered or invaded "through" or "by means of" the disobedience of the one man, Adam. "… *and death through sin…*": Sin entered into the world *through* Adam's first act of disobedience, and death entered into the world *through* sin—a devastating chain of events. It is extremely important to note that death did not enter into our world as a 'natural consequence' of sin, but as the divine penalty for sin. Death is the punishment or wages of sin (Genesis 2:17; Ezekiel 18:4; Romans 6:23).

2. "… *and so death spread to all men, because all sinned…*" *(v. 12):*

Note: "… *so death spread to all men…*": Having explained how death entered into God's world, Paul affirms what we all know to be true: death has spread to all men. Men are born dying. "… *because all sinned…*": Paul's explanation for the spread of death to all men is brief, but powerful. Death is the penalty or wage of sin (Romans 6:23), and death has spread to all men, because "all sinned." The word "sinned" in Greek is written in the aorist tense, which is often used to describe a momentary action in past time or a single event in history. In this case, the historic event to which Paul is referring is the sin and fall of Adam. According to the grammar and the context (*i.e.* the following verses), this phrase does not mean that death has spread to all men because all men personally "sin" or "have sinned," but that death has spread to all men because "all sinned" in that historic moment in the garden when Adam sinned. Through Adam's sin, all were "constituted sinners" (v. 19). For this reason, the penalty of death has spread to all men, even to infants and the like who die without having committed sin personally.

3. "… *for until the Law sin was in the world, but sin is not imputed when there is no law. Nevertheless, death reigned from Adam until Moses, even over those who had not sinned in the likeness of the offense of Adam…*" *(vs. 13-14):*

Note: These verses are given as proof of the fact that all are "made sinners" in Adam, as indicated by the way the passage begins ("for"). The logic is very clear: (1) According to the Scriptures, death is the wage of sin or the penalty for breaking God's law (v. 12; see also Romans 6:23). Only sinners or lawbreakers die. (2) Yet, countless people died before the Law of Moses was ever given, and countless infants have died in the womb even though they never personally sinned or broke God's law. (3) The death of those who have never personally sinned in the "likeness of the offense of Adam" can only be explained by the fact that the sin of Adam has been imputed to them, and they are accounted "sinners" in Adam.

4. *"… by the transgression of the one the many died…" (v. 15):*

Note: The "many" is a reference to the great mass of humanity descended from Adam. They all died. Again, Paul is showing that the penalty of death experienced by all men is *the result of the sin of one man*, namely Adam. Through his transgression alone, the many "sinned" (5:12), and therefore, the "many" died.

5. *"… judgment arose from one transgression resulting in condemnation…" (v. 16):*

Note: The word *judgment* refers to a *judicial sentence*, *decision*, or *verdict*. The word *condemnation* refers to a *damnatory sentence* or *guilty verdict*. Adam's transgression resulted in his judgment. His judgment resulted in his condemnation. The penalty for his crime was death. This condemnation and its penalty has passed on to all men, because "all sinned" in Adam.

6. *"… by the transgression of the one, death reigned through the one…" (v. 17):*

_____

_____

_____

_____

Note: Through Adam's one sin, death came to exercise absolute authority over all men (*i.e.* all men die). This is true because Adam's sin was imputed to all men and all were constituted "sinners." As sinners, they were all under the divine judgment of death. By Adam's sin, death rules and reigns throughout human history.

7. *"… through one transgression there resulted condemnation to all men…" (v. 18):*

_____

_____

_____

_____

Note: *"… through one transgression there resulted condemnation to all men…"*: This statement simply summarizes what has already been said in verses 12-17. Through the one transgression of Adam, all men were made sinners (vs. 12, 19), condemned (v. 16), and made subject to death (vs. 12, 14-15, 17).

8. *"… through the one man's disobedience the many were made sinners…" (v. 19):*

_____

_____

_____

_____

Note: The word *made* means *set down as*, *declare*, or *constitute*. As a result of Adam's disobedience, all men are now regarded and treated as sinners in a judicial sense. It is important to note that Paul does not say that as the result of Adam's sin the many were made sinful (*i.e.* born with a sinful nature), which in turn led them to live a life of sin, and come under the condemnation of death. Rather, the many were constituted sinners and thereby brought under the punishment of death even before they had the opportunity to personally sin.

MAN IS BORN IN CORRUPTION

The extreme consequence of Adam's sin was not only death, but also moral corruption: he fell from his original state of righteousness and became a morally corrupt creature. Since all men bear the guilt of Adam's sin they also bear the penalty: death and moral corruption. Every one of Adam's descendants is born under the sentence of death, morally corrupt, and wholly inclined to evil.

It is evident from every individual's experience and the collective experience of all mankind that man's moral corruption is not a learned or imitated behavior, something on the outside that works its way into the life of a man. Instead, it is an inherent trait rooted deeply in the heart, as Christ says in Mark 7:20: "That which proceeds out of the man, that is what defiles the man." Human history, secular and sacred literature, philosophy, and religion abound with illustrations of man's struggle with his own moral corruption and propensity to evil.

One of the most important phrases used by theologians to describe the depth of man's inherited moral corruption or pollution is the phrase *total depravity*. The word *depravity* comes from the Latin preposition *de* which communicates intensity and the Latin word *pravus* which means *twisted* or *crooked*. To say that something is depraved means that its original state or form has been thoroughly twisted or perverted. To say that man is depraved means that he has fallen from his original state of righteousness and that his very nature has become thoroughly corrupt. When theologians use the terms "*total*," "*pervasive*," "*holistic*," or "*radical* depravity," it is important to know what they do *not* mean and what they *do* mean:

TOTAL DEPRAVITY DOES **NOT** MEAN...

1. ... *that the image of God in man was totally lost in the fall.* In Genesis 9:6, I Corinthians 11:7, and James 3:9, the Scripture still refers to man as being in the image of God. Therefore, there is a real sense in which the image of God remains in every man.

2. ... *that man has no knowledge of the person and will of God.* The Scriptures teach us that all men know enough of the true God to hate Him and know enough of His truth to reject it and attempt to restrain it (Romans 1:18, 30).

3. ... *that man does not possess a conscience or that he is totally* **insensible** *to good and evil.* In Romans 2:14-15, the Scriptures teach that all men possess a conscience. If not seared (I Timothy 4:1-2), such a conscience may lead men to admire virtuous character and actions.

4. ... *that man is incapable of demonstrating virtue.* There are men who love their families, sacrifice their own lives to save others, and perform great acts of generosity and altruism. It is recognized that men are capable of loving others, civic duty, and even external religious good (Matthew 7:11).

5. ... *that all men are as immoral or wicked as they could be, that all men are equally immoral, or that all men indulge in every form of evil that exists.* Not all men are delinquents, fornicators, or murderers, but all are capable of such (Jeremiah 17:9; Matthew 5:21-30). That which restrains them is the grace of God (Psalm 81:11-12; Acts 7:41-42; Romans 1:18-32; II Thessalonians 2:5-12; II Peter 2:15-16).

TOTAL DEPRAVITY **DOES** MEAN...

1. ... *that the image of God in man has been seriously defaced, or disfigured, and that moral corruption has polluted the entire person*—body (Romans 6:6, 12; 7:24; 8:10, 13), reason (Romans 1:21; II Corinthians 3:14-15; 4:3-4; Ephesians 4:17-19), emotions (Romans 1:26-27; Galatians 5:24; II Timothy 3:1-5), and will (Romans 6:17; 8:7-8).

2. ... *that the mind of man is hostile toward God, cannot subject itself to the will of God, and cannot please God* (Romans 8:7-8).

3. ... *that everything men do is contaminated by their own moral corruption.* Man's moral corruption and sin pervade his most commendable deeds (Isaiah 64:6).

4. ... *that the deeds of man are not prompted by any love for God or any desire to obey His commands.* No man loves God in a worthy manner or as the law commands (Deuteronomy 6:4-5; Matthew 22:35-37), nor is there a man who glorifies God in every thought, word, and deed (I Corinthians 10:31; Romans 1:21). All men prefer self to God (II Timothy 3:1-5). All the acts of altruism, heroics, civic duty, and external religious good are prompted by the love of self but not the love of God.

5. ... *that man is born with a great propensity or inclination towards sin.* All men are capable of the greatest evil, the most unspeakable crimes, and the most shameful perversions (Jeremiah 17:9; Matthew 5:18-19).

6. ... *that mankind is inclined to greater and greater moral corruption, and this deterioration would be even more rapid than it is if it were not for the grace of God which restrains the evil of men* (Psalm 81:11-12; Acts 7:41-42; Romans 1:18-32; II Thessalonians 2:5-12; II Timothy 2:16; II Peter 2:15-16).

7. ... *that man cannot free himself from his sinful and depraved condition.* He is spiritually dead (Ephesians 2:1-3), morally corrupt (Genesis 8:21), and cannot change himself (Jeremiah 13:23).

Now that we have summarized the meaning of total depravity, we will consider the teaching of Scripture. We will find abundant testimony to what we have learned: *since all men bear the guilt of Adam's sin they also bear the penalty of death and share in his moral corruption.* Every one of Adam's descendants is born morally corrupt and wholly inclined to evil.

1. Through a careful study of **Genesis 5:1-3**—which describes events *after the fall*— we will clearly see the devastating consequences of Adam's sin and the spread of moral corruption throughout the human race. Read the text until you are familiar with its contents and then answer the following questions:

   a. *According to **Genesis 5:1**, in whose image was Adam made?*

   _____

   _____

   _____

   _____

   b. *According to **Genesis 5:3**, in whose likeness were Adam's descendents made? Explain the significance of this truth:*

   _____

   _____

   _____

   _____

Note: Adam was made in the image of God, but the descendants of Adam were made in the fallen and depraved image of Adam. It is important to note that men do not merely inherit Adam's moral corruption in the same way that a son might inherit a physical trait or deformity from his father. The moral corruption of Adam's descendants is a result of God's judgment against them: Adam sinned and came under the penalty of death and moral corruption. Adam's sin has been imputed to all his descendants and therefore they are subject to the same penalty: death and corruption.

2. Since the fall of Adam, all men are born with a morally corrupt nature that is void of good, hostile toward God, and inclined to evil. What do the following Scriptures teach about this truth? How do they demonstrate that man's moral corruption is not a learned behavior, but a reflection of his very nature?

Genesis 8:21

Note: The word *youth* refers to one's early life or childhood. There is no need to teach a child to be selfish or self-centered, to lie, to manipulate, etc. Such sinful attitudes and deeds spring forth from his very nature.

Psalm 58:3

Psalm 51:5

Note: This does *not* mean that the sexual relations between David's parents that lead to his birth were sinful. God commanded that men multiply and bring forth children (Genesis 1:28). And even if David's parents had conceived him by committing an adulterous or otherwise wicked act, this does not explain the phrase, "I was brought forth in iniquity"—the act of giving birth is not wicked, even if the child was conceived immorally. The only explanation of this verse is that David is describing what Adam's fall has done to man. David is simply putting forth a truth that is defended in the Scriptures and demonstrated in the history of mankind: man's moral corruption and propensity to evil is not merely a learned behavior, but a part of his very being or nature.

3. Having established the truth that all men are born bearing the moral corruption of Adam, we will now consider the Scriptures that illustrate the severity or depth of this moral corruption. What do the following Scriptures teach us about the depth and extension of man's corruption?

Genesis 6:5 (before the flood); 8:21 (after the flood)

Note: To illustrate the point, suppose that one could place on a video all the thoughts of a man from his earliest moments in childhood to the present day, and then show that film to his closest friends and family, to those with whom he had shared his most intimate thoughts and weaknesses. It would be no exaggeration to say that he would be so overcome with shame that he would never be able to face them again. Amazingly, even the evil and hard-hearted man who produced such vile thoughts would be terrified and overcome by the extent of his own moral corruption.

Job 15:14-16

Job 25:4-6

_____

_____

_____

_____

_____

Ecclesiastes 9:3

_____

_____

_____

_____

_____

Isaiah 64:6

_____

_____

_____

_____

_____

Note: The greatest, most commendable deeds of men are nothing but filthy rags before God. One might clothe a leper in the finest, white silk to cover his sores, but immediately the corruption of his flesh would bleed through the garment, leaving it as vile as the man it seeks to hide. So are the 'good works' of men before God. They bear the corruption of the man who does them.

4. When speaking about the moral corruption of man, special attention must be given to the heart. In the Scriptures, the heart refers to the seat of the mind, will, and emotions. It represents the very core and essence of one's being and person. According to the Scriptures, the very heart of man is corrupt and from it flows every form of sin, rebellion, and perversity. Answer the following questions to complete the exercise:

   a. *How is the heart of man described in **Jeremiah 17:9**?*

_____

_____

_____

b. *According to **Matthew 15:19-20** and **Mark 7:20-23**, how does the corrupt heart of man affect all that a man is and does?*

5. To conclude this part of our study on the moral corruption of man, we will consider a brief but powerful statement made by the Lord Jesus Christ in **Matthew 7:11**. What is this statement and how does it demonstrate Christ's strong belief in the moral depravity of man?

"If you then, being E_____..."

6. Based upon the Scriptures we have studied in questions 1-5, summarize what you have learned about man's moral corruption:

"AND YOU WERE DEAD IN YOUR TRESPASSES AND SINS, IN WHICH
YOU FORMERLY WALKED ACCORDING TO THE COURSE OF THIS
WORLD, ACCORDING TO THE PRINCE OF THE POWER OF THE
AIR, OF THE SPIRIT THAT IS NOW WORKING IN THE SONS OF
DISOBEDIENCE. AMONG THEM WE TOO ALL FORMERLY LIVED IN
THE LUSTS OF OUR FLESH, INDULGING THE DESIRES OF THE FLESH
AND OF THE MIND, AND WERE BY NATURE CHILDREN
OF WRATH, EVEN AS THE REST."

– EPHESIANS 2:1-3 –

SPIRITUAL DEATH

THE MEANING OF SPIRITUAL DEATH

An important phrase used by theologians to describe the depth of man's moral corruption is *spiritual death*. According to the Scriptures, the divine judgment that fell upon Adam not only resulted in his physical death, but also his spiritual death. This means that he became responsive to every sort of wicked stimuli, both human and demonic, but unresponsive to the person and will of God. Just as a man is declared dead the moment he ceases to respond to all forms of stimuli, so also fallen man is declared spiritually dead because of his absolute inability to respond to God.

The Scriptures teach us that this aspect of the divine judgment that fell upon Adam was not limited to him alone, but includes the entire race of humanity. Every human being is born into this world as a spiritual stillborn, void of true spiritual life toward God and unresponsive to the person and will of God. In order for fallen man to respond to God in love and obedience, a spiritual resurrection must occur through the supernatural working of God's grace and power.

1. In **Ephesians 2:1-3** is found one of Scripture's most revealing descriptions of the spiritual death of fallen man. Read the text several times until you are familiar with its contents. Afterward, explain in your own words the meaning of each verse:

a. *"And you were dead in your trespasses and sins…" (v. 1):*

_____

_____

_____

_____

Note: This verse affirms that man is *spiritually dead* and that this state of death is characterized by a life of "trespasses and sins." It is important to note that this dead condition, which entered the human race through Adam's one act of sin, has subsequently been absolutely universal among his descendents. Men and women add to this vile and corrupt condition by their own willful sin (see Galatians 6:8: "For the one who sows to his own flesh will from the flesh reap corruption…").

b. *"… in which you formerly walked according to the course of this world…" (v. 2):*

_____

_____

_____

_____

Note: Prior to conversion, every person 'walks in' or 'practices' sin as a style of life. They do not walk according to the will of God, but according to the way of a fallen world that is hostile toward God and disobedient.

c. *"… according to the prince of the power of the air, of the spirit that is now working in the sons of disobedience." (v. 2):*

_____

_____

_____

_____

Note: Prior to conversion, not only does every person walk in the ways of a fallen humanity, but also, they live in a way that conforms to the will of the devil. This is a frightening truth!

d. *"Among them we too all formerly lived in the lusts of our flesh, indulging the desires of the flesh and of the mind…" (v. 3):*

Note: Prior to conversion, every person without exception is driven, or led about, by the lusts of their flesh (*i.e.* the wicked desires of their fallen humanity that is hostile toward God and rebellious). They indulge their wicked desires and thoughts.

e. *"… and were by nature children of wrath, even as the rest." (v. 3):*

Note: Prior to conversion, God's wrath abides upon a person (John 3:36). It is important to understand that the wrath of God is not directed towards a person simply because of what they do, but also because of what they are. Man's fallen and evil nature evokes the wrath of God.

2. In **Genesis 2:17**, Adam received a warning from God about the dreadful consequence of disobedience. According to this text, what would occur the day that Adam violated God's command? What does this text teach us about the spiritual death that Adam incurred as the result of his sin?

Note: The penalty for Adam's sin was death. This death was not only physical, but also spiritual. It was absolute, certain, and unavoidable that humanity would experience this spiritual death as a result of Adam's transgression. They became responsive to every sort of wicked stimuli, both human and demonic, but *unresponsive* to the person and will of God.

3. In **Ephesians 4:17-19** is found still another important description of the spiritual death that abides in the heart of every man prior to conversion. Read the text several times until you are familiar with its contents. Afterward, explain the meaning of each of the following truths:

a. *"[Fallen men walk] in the futility of their mind, being darkened in their understanding…"* *(vs. 17-18):*

_____

_____

_____

_____

> **Note:** The *mind* of the spiritually dead may be able to accomplish great endeavors in science, architecture, literature, etc., but with regard to God it is empty of truth and filled with all sorts of vanities, heresies, and contradictions. When fallen men seek to be 'spiritual' or 'religious,' the results are catastrophic, even absurd. This is true because their minds are futile and darkened.

b. *"… excluded from the life of God…"* *(v. 18):*

_____

_____

_____

_____

> **Note:** As shown in our previous lessons, Adam enjoyed perfect fellowship with God and walked in His favor and grace before the Fall. But after his fall into sin, as God's righteous judgment upon humanity, the Lord withdrew His good favor and expelled them from His life-giving presence. According to this statement by the apostle Paul, all men continue in this state, excluded from the life of God (and the joy and virtue He brings) unless God mercifully intervenes to save.

c. *"… because of the ignorance that is in them, because of the hardness of their heart…"* *(v. 18):*

_____

_____

_____

Note: It is important to understand that man is not a victim who is separated from God because of some unavoidable ignorance that he cannot help. Man's ignorance is *self-imposed*. He is hostile towards God and does not want to know Him or His will. Man is ignorant of spiritual things because he closes his eyes and refuses to look at God. He covers his ears and refuses to listen.

d. *"… they, having become callous, have given themselves over to sensuality for the practice of every kind of impurity with greediness." (v. 19):*

Note: In hardening his heart against God, fallen man becomes callous to all spiritual truth and virtue. He then voluntarily gives himself over to the very evil that God opposes.

4. In the Scriptures, there are several descriptions of fallen man's spiritual death that illustrate what it means to be "spiritually dead." Complete each declaration by filling in the blanks and then explain its meaning:

   a. *Fallen men are D_____ even while they L_____ (I Timothy 5:6).*

Note: Prior to conversion, man is a spiritual corpse—physically alive, but spiritually dead. He is dead to the reality of God and His will.

   b. *Fallen men have a name that they are A_____, but they are D_____ (Revelation 3:1).*

Note: Prior to conversion, a man may appear very religious and even God-fearing, but all his works are external and motivated by self-love. In his heart, he does not love God, nor does he seek God's glory. The fact is, he is spiritually dead, in spite of his assertion to the contrary.

c. *Fallen men have hearts of S_____ (Ezekiel 11:19).*

Note: A statue of stone is inanimate and is unresponsive to any sort of stimulus. One can pinch, poke, or prod a statue, and yet it will not respond. In the same way, the heart of fallen man will not respond to divine stimuli. It is as dead as a stone to God.

d. *Fallen men are like A_____ trees without F_____, D_____ dead, U_____ (Jude 12).*

Note: It would be difficult to find a more graphic illustration of man's spiritual deadness. Prior to conversion, there is no spiritual life in a man.

e. *Fallen men perform religious duties and rituals that God considers to be D_____ works (Hebrews 6:1; 9:14).*

_____

_____

_____

Note: Again, prior to conversion, a man may appear very religious, but all his works are external and motivated by self-love. He is as fruitless as a dead tree.

"... HOW CAN YOU, BEING EVIL, SPEAK WHAT IS GOOD?"

– MATTHEW 12:34-35 –

MORAL INABILITY

THE MEANING OF MORAL INABILITY

Moral inability is another term that is commonly employed by Bible students to describe the extent of man's moral corruption or radical depravity. This doctrine teaches us that fallen man is *unable* to love, obey, or please God.

Upon hearing of such a doctrine, one may ask, "How is man responsible before God if he is *unable* to do anything that God commands?" The answer is very important. If man did not love or obey God because he lacked the mental faculties to do so, or was somehow physically restrained, then it would indeed be unfair for God to hold him accountable. He would be a victim. However, this is not the case with man. His inability is moral and stems from his hostility toward God. Man is *unable* to love God because he *hates* God. He is *unable* to obey God because he *disdains* His commands. *He is unable to please God because he does not hold the glory and good pleasure of God to be a worthy goal.* Man is not a victim, but a culprit. He *cannot*, because he *will not*. His corruption and enmity toward God are so great that he would rather suffer eternal perdition than acknowledge God to be God and submit to His sovereignty. For this reason, *moral inability* may also be called *willing hostility*. A wonderful example of moral inability or willing hostility is found in Genesis 37:4:

> *"His [i.e. Joseph's] brothers saw that their father loved him more than all his brothers; and so they hated him and could not speak to him on friendly terms."*

Joseph's brothers could not speak to him on friendly terms. It is not because they lacked the physical ability to speak (*i.e.* they were not mute), but because their hatred was so great toward him that they were unwilling to be friendly to him. In the same way, fallen man's hostility toward God is so great he cannot bring himself to submit to God.

The Bondage of the Will

Man's will is an expression of his nature. If man possessed a morally pure nature, then his will would be inclined to perform acts that were morally pure. If man were holy and righteous, he would love a holy and righteous God and would love and obey His commands. However, fallen man possesses a morally corrupt nature, and so his will is inclined to performing acts that are as morally corrupt as his heart. Fallen man is unholy and unrighteous. Therefore, he hates a holy and righteous God, fights against His truth, and refuses to submit to His commands. Here we find the answer to the often-debated question:

Does man possess a free will?

The Scriptural answer is that man is 'free' to choose as he pleases, but because his very nature is morally depraved, it pleases him to turn away from the good and choose evil, to hate truth and believe a lie, to deny God and fight against His will. In one sense, fallen man does have a 'free will,' but he does *not* have a 'good will.' Therefore, he will always 'freely' choose in opposition to the person and will of God. Man cannot escape what he is. He is by nature evil, and he performs works of evil 'willfully' and 'freely.'

1. In **Matthew 7:16-20** is found an excellent illustration of the truth that man's will is an expression of his nature. Read the text several times until you are familiar with its contents and then explain the meaning of each phrase.

    a. *"You will know them by their fruits. Grapes are not gathered from thorn bushes nor figs from thistles, are they?" (v. 16):*

Note: We identify the nature of a tree by the fruit that it bears. In the same way, the true nature or character of a man is revealed, not by what he confesses, but by what he does.

b. *"So every good tree bears good fruit, but the bad tree bears bad fruit." (v. 17):*

Note: There is a direct and undeniable relationship between the nature of a tree and the fruit that it bears. The same is true of a man's nature and his works. A corrupt nature can only produce corrupt works.

c. *"A good tree cannot produce bad fruit, nor can a bad tree produce good fruit." (v. 18):*

d. *"Every tree that does not bear good fruit is cut down and thrown into the fire." (v. 19):*

e. *"So then, you will know them by their fruits." (v. 20):*

2. In **Matthew 12:34-35** is found still another excellent illustration of fallen man's moral inability. Read the text several times until you are familiar with its contents and then explain the meaning of each of the following phrases.

a. *"You brood of vipers, how can you, being evil, speak what is good?" (v. 34):*

_____

_____

_____

_____

Note: One would be hard-pressed to find a greater example of moral inability than that which is found here in the teachings of our Lord Jesus Christ.

b. *"For the mouth speaks out of that which fills the heart." (v. 34):*

_____

_____

_____

_____

Note: In the Scriptures, there is always a direct relationship between a man's heart or nature, and his words and works. Man wills, speaks, and acts in accordance with his nature.

c. *"The good man brings out of his good treasure what is good; and the evil man brings out of his evil treasure what is evil." (v. 35):*

_____

_____

_____

_____

FALLEN MAN "CANNOT LOVE" GOD

Most, even the irreligious, claim some degree of love or affection toward God, and very rarely would we ever encounter an individual so bold as to confess their hatred toward Him. Nevertheless, the Scriptures testify that fallen man *cannot* love

God. In fact, all of Adam's race hates God and lives at war against Him. Most who claim a genuine love for God know very little about His attributes and works as they are revealed in the Scripture. Therefore the 'god' they love is nothing more than a figment of their imagination. They have made a 'god' in their own image, and they love what they have made. As God declares in Psalm 50:21, "You thought that I was just like you; I will reprove you...."

If fallen men who claim to love God were to investigate the Scriptures, they would most certainly find a God much different than that which is presently the object of their affections. If they went on to study the attributes of God, such as holiness, justice, sovereignty, and wrath, they would most likely respond in disgust and declare, "My God's not like that!" or "I could never love a God like that!" We would quickly see that when fallen man is confronted with the true God of the Scriptures, his only reaction is hatred and hostility! What is the reason for this adverse reaction? Again, it has to do with who man is *at the very core of his being*. If man were by nature holy and righteous, then he could easily love a holy and righteous God and would joyfully submit to His laws. However, man is by nature depraved and corrupt, and therefore he cannot!

1. What descriptions of fallen man are given in the following Scriptures? What do they communicate to us about his moral corruption and hostility toward God?

   a. *H_____ of God (**Romans 1:30**).*

   _____

   _____

   _____

   _____

   _____

   b. *E_____ of God (**Romans 5:10**).*

   _____

   _____

   _____

   _____

2. Why would any rational creature hate the very God who brought it into existence and selflessly sustains it? Why does fallen man hate God and live at enmity against Him? What do the following Scriptures tell us?

John 3:19-20; Colossians 1:21

II Timothy 3:4

Romans 8:7

According to the Scriptures listed above, fallen man hates his good and benevolent God to whom he owes his all, because: (1) He loves evil and is engaged in evil deeds. He does not come to God for fear that his evil deeds might be exposed. (2) He loves sinful pleasures rather than God. (3) His mind is depraved and set on the flesh (*i.e.* it is morally corrupt and strongly desires the very things that a holy and righteous God opposes).

FALLEN MAN "CANNOT KNOW" THE THINGS OF GOD

Through God's gracious providence, the human race has gained great intellectual achievements in science, technology, medicine, etc. Nevertheless, fallen man's knowledge of God is nothing more than a twisted maze of heresy and futile thinking. This ignorance is not the result of a 'hidden God,' but of a 'hiding man.' God has clearly revealed Himself to men through creation, His sovereign works in history, the Scriptures, and finally through His incarnate Son. Man, being spiritually dead and morally corrupt, has responded to this revelation by closing his eyes and covering his ears. He *cannot* know the truth, because he hates the truth, and seeks to repress it. He hates the truth because it is God's truth, and it speaks against him. Therefore, he cannot bear to hear it.

1. According to **I Corinthians 2:14**, can fallen man understand the things of God taught by the Holy Spirit? Explain your answer:

_____

_____

_____

_____

2. In the first part of our study on moral inability, we learned that man cannot love God because of his hostility toward *God Himself*. Now we will see that man's hostility toward God is also reflected in his opposition to *God's truth*. It is important to understand that men are not helpless victims who genuinely desire spiritual truth, but cannot obtain it. Rather, they hate the truth and do all that is in their power to deny and repress it. What do the following Scriptures teach us about this truth?

Job 21:14-15

_____

_____

_____

_____

Romans 1:18

_____

_____

_____

_____

Note: The word *suppress* comes from a Greek word that may also be translated, *restrain, hinder, detain,* or *hold back.*

3. In **Romans 1:21-32**, we find an important description of humanity's hostility toward God and His truth. Fallen man is not a victim who desires the truth of God but does not have the faculties to know it. Rather he is a *hater of the truth* who

does not want to know it. Read the text several times until you are familiar with its contents. Afterward, explain the following verses:

a. *"For even though they knew God, they did not honor Him as God or give thanks…"* (v. 21):

_____

_____

_____

_____

b. *"… but they became futile in their speculations, and their foolish heart was darkened."* (v. 21):

_____

_____

_____

_____

c. *"Professing to be wise, they became fools…"* (v. 22):

_____

_____

_____

_____

d. *"… and exchanged the glory of the incorruptible God for an image in the form of corruptible man and of birds and four-footed animals and crawling creatures."* (v. 23):

_____

_____

_____

_____

e. *"For they exchanged the truth of God for a lie…"* (v. 25):

_____

_____

f. *"… and worshiped and served the creature rather than the Creator, who is blessed forever. Amen." (v. 25):*

FALLEN MAN "CANNOT OBEY OR PLEASE" GOD

There is one great common denominator between all religions outside of Christianity—they all believe that a right standing with God is based upon obedience, personal merit, or some ability to please God. Christianity stands alone in declaring that man is hopelessly and helplessly lost. He *cannot improve* his standing before God, he *cannot obey* God, and he *cannot please* God. If he is to be saved, God alone must save him. It is this one truth that fallen man hates most of all, for it requires him to humble himself before God, acknowledge his sin, and ask for mercy!

In **Romans 8:7-8** is one of Scripture's most important descriptions of man's moral inability. Read the text several times until you are familiar with its contents and then explain what each phrase teaches us about man's inability to obey or please God:

1. *"… because the mind set on the flesh is hostile toward God…" (v. 7):*

Note: The "mind set on the flesh" refers to the mind of fallen man who is still in an unconverted state, unregenerate, and without Christ (see vs. 1-6).

2. *"… for it does not subject itself to the law of God…" (v. 7):*

3. *"... for it is not even able to do so..." (v. 7):*

_____

_____

_____

_____

4. *"... and those who are in the flesh cannot please God." (v. 8):*

_____

_____

_____

_____

Note: Paul's description of man's inability in this passage is striking. It is not just that fallen man cannot please God, but that he cannot please God because his mind is "set on the flesh" and because he is "in the flesh." Fallen man is bent on fulfilling the desires of his flesh. He is so passionately absorbed with these lusts, so blinded by them, and so full of hatred for whomever suggests that he live for something higher, that loving and serving God is impossible.

FALLEN MAN "CANNOT SEEK" GOD

We live in a world full of self-proclaimed 'seekers after God,' and yet the Scriptures destroy all such boasting with one simple declaration: "there is none who seeks for God" (Romans 3:11). Quite often we hear young converts to Christianity who begin their testimony with the words, "For years I was seeking after God," but the Scriptures again reply, "there is none who seeks for God." Man is an utterly fallen creature whose nature is depraved and perverse. He hates a holy God and opposes His truth because it convicts him of his depravity and rebellion. He will not come to God but will do absolutely everything in his power to escape Him and forget Him. God is righteous and man is a lawbreaker, therefore he is no more inclined to seek God than a criminal at large is inclined to seek an officer of the law.

1. Often we hear men claim to be 'seekers of the truth' or 'seekers of God,' but how does Scripture respond to such claims?

    a. *According to **Romans 1:18**, does fallen man sincerely seek the truth?*

    b. *According to **Romans 3:11** does fallen man sincerely seek God?*

2. We have learned that fallen man will not seek God. Why does man have such an aversion to God? Why will fallen man not seek Him? What does **John 3:19-20** teach us?

3. The Scriptures teach us that fallen man *will not* and *cannot* seek God. According to the teachings of Jesus in **John 6:44** and **John 6:65**, what must happen before a man can seek God and His salvation?

FALLEN MAN "CANNOT CHANGE OR REFORM" HIMSELF

The twentieth century began with great optimism about man's ability to evolve into a greater, nobler creature. It was supposed to be the age of reform, but it ended in a pitiful stupor of despair and confusion. The Scriptures clearly teach that man is born spiritually dead and morally depraved. Any and every human effort at reformation is hopeless. Any and every attempt to make oneself pleasing or acceptable to God will end in utter failure. Man has only one hope—the mercy and grace of God.

Having established man's inability to love, obey, or please God, we will now consider what the Scriptures teach about man's inability to change, reform himself, or make himself right before God. What do the following Scriptures teach us about this truth?

Job 14:4

_____

_____

_____

_____

Jeremiah 2:22

_____

_____

_____

_____

Jeremiah 13:23

_____

_____

_____

_____

"... THE WHOLE WORLD LIES IN THE POWER OF THE EVIL ONE."

– I John 5:19 –

ENSLAVEMENT TO SATAN

Before we go on to study the character and universality of sin, it is important that we consider fallen man's relationship to Satan. We will see that fallen man is not only alienated from God, but also united to Satan in his hostility and rebellion against God.

In the beginning, Adam was free to obey God and exercise dominion over all the earth. As a result of his rebellion against God, both he and his race fell into corruption and slavery. Since the fall, every son and daughter of Adam is born in bondage to sin and in slavery to Satan. Although few men would ever regard themselves to be 'followers' of the devil, the Scripture testifies that all are born under his dominion and are held captive by him to do his will. Although it is proper to use the term 'enslavement,' we must understand that man is not a victim held against his will. Fallen man has rejected the rule of God and given himself over to the rule of Satan.

THE RULE OF SATAN

We must be very careful whenever we speak about the rule and power of Satan. God and the devil are *not* equal powers locked in some cosmic struggle to win the universe. The devil is a finite creature whom God created and over whom God rules with absolute sovereignty. Although Satan's rebellion against God is his own doing, it has been ordained and permitted by God for God's purposes and glory.

Without denying or diminishing the truth of God's absolute sovereignty, we can say that there is a very real sense in which this present fallen world and its fallen inhabitants lie in the power of the Evil One. To this truth, the Scriptures bear abundant witness.

1. In **Luke 4:5-6**, Satan makes a declaration about himself and his relationship to this fallen world. What does he declare and what does it mean?

   _____

   _____

   _____

   _____

   > **Note:** It is important to note two things: First, Jesus did not contest the devil's claim. There is a real sense in which Satan has dominion in this world (I John 5:19). Secondly, the domain of which the devil boasted had been "handed over" to him. The devil's rule is both permitted and limited by God.

2. It is important to understand that Satan's declaration in Luke 4:6 is no idle boast. What does **I John 5:19** teach us about this truth?

   _____

   _____

   _____

   _____

   > **Note:** The Scripture declares that this fallen world and its fallen inhabitants are held firmly in the devil's grip. As fallen man seeks his independence from God, he unwittingly makes himself a slave to Satan. This is a frightening truth.

3. In the Scriptures, a title is important in that it often communicates something about the nature of the person who bears it. What are the titles given to Satan in the following Scriptures?

   a. *The R_____ of this W_____ (John 12:31; 14:30; 16:11).* God is the absolute Sovereign over all things, and yet there is a real sense in which dominion has been given to Satan to rule over this fallen world. With such a ruler, is there any wonder why this present age is filled with such evil and fallen man suffers such misery?

b. *The G____ of this W_____ (II Corinthians 4:4).* It is the sure testimony of Scripture that there is only one true God. But in this passage, Satan is referred to as the "god of this world" in the sense that he is working with great power in this present evil age, and fallen men have made him their "god" and live according to his will.

c. *The P_____ of the P_____ of the A___ (Ephesians 2:2).* Satan is a spirit and unhindered by the material restraints of man. His power and authority go far beyond any "earthbound" prince.

SATAN AND FALLEN MAN

Both Satan and men are fallen creatures, and there is great affinity between them (*i.e.* they have much in common). They are alike in their moral corruption and in their enmity against God. Although it is repulsive to most, it is nevertheless true: there is such a moral likeness between fallen man and Satan that, prior to conversion, all men are not only his *subjects* but also his *children*.

1. We have learned from our study of the Scriptures that Satan is described as both a ruler and a god over Adam's fallen race, and he works effectively among them. According to the following Scriptures, how is fallen man described? Fill in the blank and then write your thoughts.

   a. *Fallen man is a C_____ of the D_____ (John 8:44; 1 John 3:8-10).*

   _____

   _____

   _____

   _____

> **Note:** While all men are the special creation of God's handiwork, and in that sense His children (Acts 17:24-29), the Scriptures deny any further sense of the universal fatherhood of God. In fact, Jesus authoritatively divides Adam's race into two categories: (1) The children of the devil are those who refuse God's offer of mercy and remain in their rebellion. They show themselves to be children of the devil in that they practice the sinful works of the devil. (2) The children of God are those who receive God's forgiveness and the adoption of sons through the atoning death of Jesus Christ. They show themselves to be the children of God in that they practice the righteous works of their heavenly Father.

b. *Fallen man lives under the D_____ of S_____ (Acts 26:18; see also* **Colossians 1:13**).

_____

_____

_____

_____

Note: The word *dominion* refers to the *power, authority,* or *jurisdiction* of Satan. To live under Satan's dominion is to live under his rule, government, and controlling influence.

c. *Fallen man lives A_____ to the P_____ of the power of the air* **(Ephesians 2:2)**.

_____

_____

_____

_____

d. *Fallen man is caught in the S_____ of the D_____ (II Timothy 2:26)*.

_____

_____

_____

_____

Note: A snare or noose was a type of trap used in ancient times to catch birds and other animals. It was a hidden device that would entangle an animal unexpectedly and suddenly. It serves as an excellent illustration of Satan's deadly work.

e. *Fallen man is held C_____to do the devil's W_____ (II Timothy 2:26)*.

_____

_____

_____

_____

Note: Satan captures men in order to enslave them and use them to carry out his will in this fallen world. True, very few people would say that they serve the devil and do his will, and most will either laugh at this claim or become enraged upon hearing it. But it is the teaching of Scripture that refusal to serve God results in serving Satan. Fallen man is therefore like a horse, and his rider is the devil. Whatever the devil commands, fallen man does, whether he admits it or not—he is being led by another, whether he knows it or not.

2. We have learned from our study of the Scriptures that Satan is described as both a ruler and a god over Adam's fallen race. According to the following Scriptures, how does he work among fallen man? How is it that he makes them his subjects and enslaves them to do his will?

   a. *Satan masks his true identity (**II Corinthians 11:14-15**).*

   b. *Satan lies (**John 8:44**) and deceives (**Revelation 12:9**).*

   c. *Satan blinds fallen man to the truth (**II Corinthians 4:4**).*

   d. *Satan tempts (**Matthew 4:1-3; I Thessalonians 3:5**).*

"... BOTH JEWS AND GREEKS ARE ALL UNDER SIN; AS IT IS WRITTEN, 'THERE IS NONE RIGHTEOUSNESS, NOT EVEN ONE; THERE IS NONE WHO UNDERSTANDS, THERE IS NONE WHO SEEKS FOR GOD; ALL HAVE TURNED ASIDE, TOGETHER THEY HAVE BECOME USELESS; THERE IS NONE WHO DOES GOOD, THERE IS NOT EVEN ONE.'"

– ROMANS 3:9-12 –

"THE WAY OF THE WICKED IS AN ABOMINATION TO THE LORD..."

– PROVERBS 15:9 –

THE CHARACTER AND UNIVERSALITY OF SIN

THE SINFULNESS OF SIN

To begin our study of man's personal participation in Adam's rebellion, we must have a correct understanding of the nature or character of sin. Therefore it is necessary that we study several prominent attributes and manifestations of sin as they are revealed in the Scriptures. In doing so, we will discover that sin is much more than an error in moral judgment, even much more than disobedience to some impersonal law. Sin is a crime against the person of God. In our study we must do more than simply define terms. We must regain a biblical understanding of the *sinfulness of sin*. We live in a world and worship in churches that, for the most part, no longer understand the heinous nature of sin, and so we must endeavor to rediscover what has been lost. *Our understanding of God and of the greatness of our salvation in Christ depends upon it.*

SIN IS ALWAYS AGAINST GOD

Sin is always first and foremost a sin against God and an affront to His person. To disobey a divine command is to clench the fist and shake it in the face the One who gives life to and rules over all men. Today, if people speak of sin at all, they speak of sin against man, or sin against society, or even sin against nature, but rarely do we hear of sin against God. A person is thought to be good because they have good relations with their fellowman, even though they live in total disregard for God and His will. People often ask how God can judge an atheist who is a good man, but they ask this because they are blind to the fact that a man cannot be good if he denies his Creator and renders nothing to the One who gives him all good things. The Scriptures record that King David lied to his people, committed adultery, and even orchestrated the murder of an innocent man (II Samuel 11-12). And yet when confronted with his sins, he cried out to God, "Against You, You only, I have sinned and done what is evil in Your sight" (Psalm 51:4). David knew that all sin is first and foremost sin against God. Until one understands this truth, one can never understand the heinous nature of sin.

Sin is Failure to Love God

The greatest of all sins is the violation of the greatest of all commands: "And you shall love the Lord your God with all your heart, and with all your soul, and with all your mind, and with all your strength" (Mark 12:28-30). Christ declared, "If you love Me, you will keep My commandments" (John 14:15). Therefore, all disobedience is a demonstration of our lack of love toward God. For this reason, when the apostle Paul sought to prove the depravity of mankind in the first three chapters of the book of Romans, he referred to Adam's race as "haters of God" (Romans 1:30). No greater indictment could be made against fallen man. Not loving God is at the very heart of all rebellion. It should also be noted that a man might be very religious and conscientious of divine law and duty and yet be a terrible sinner before God, if his obedience is prompted by anything other than love for God.

Sin is Failure to Glorify God

The Scriptures declare that man was created for the glory of God and that all that man does, even the most menial tasks of eating and drinking, should be done for God's glory (I Corinthians 10:31). For man to glorify God is for him to esteem the supremacy and worth of God above all things, to take joy in God and be satisfied in Him above all things, and to live before God with the reverence, gratitude, and worship that is due Him. Sin is the very opposite of glorifying God. When man sins he becomes the opposite of what he was created to be. A sinful man is a creature who has dislocated himself and perverted the very reason for his existence. He has replaced *God* with *self* and *God's will* with *self-will*. The apostle Paul writes that "though they knew God, they did not honor Him as God" (Romans 1:21) and that "they exchanged the truth of God for a lie, and worshipped and served the creature rather than the Creator, who is blessed forever. Amen" (Romans 1:25). Sin's roots go much deeper than what is seen on the surface: it is man's refusal to acknowledge God's right *as God*. It is man's determination to set himself above his Creator, usurp His throne, and steal His glory. Sin is fundamentally a refusal to glorify God as God, and it manifests itself anytime that man seeks his own glory above God's.

SIN IS GODLESS AND UNGODLY

The word *godlessness* denotes a refusal to acknowledge God as God, a desire to live a 'godless' existence, *free from His sovereignty and law*. The word *ungodliness* denotes a refusal to be conformed to the character and will of God, *a desire for moral depravity rather than likeness to God*. It has been said that the greatest compliment that may be paid to another person is to desire to be *with* them and be *like* them. Sin reveals an inward desire to live *without* God and to be *unlike* God. This is a great affront to Him!

SIN IS REBELLION AND INSUBORDINATION

In I Samuel 15:23, the Scriptures declare: "For rebellion is as the sin of divination, and insubordination is as iniquity and idolatry." The word *rebellion* is translated from the Hebrew word *meri*, which means *contentious, rebellious,* or *disobedient toward*. The word *insubordination* is translated from the Hebrew word *patsar,* which literally means *to press* or *to push*. It denotes one that is pushy, insolent, arrogant, and presumptuous. There are no small sins, because all sin is rebellion and insubordination. According to I Samuel 15:23, to practice any form of rebellion is as evil as partaking in a pagan or demonic ritual, and to practice any form of insubordination is as evil as partaking in gross iniquity or rendering worship to a false god.

SIN IS LAWLESSNESS

In I John 3:4, the Scriptures declare, "Everyone who practices sin also practices lawlessness; and sin is lawlessness." The word *lawlessness* is translated from the Greek word *anomia* [*a*, without, no + *nomos*, law]. To practice *lawlessness* is to live *without law* or as though God had never revealed His will to mankind. A person may *practice lawlessness* by openly defying the rule and law of God, or by simply being unconcerned and willingly ignorant. In either case, the person is showing contempt for God and His law. The abominable nature of *practicing lawlessness* is seen in the fact that the *antichrist* is referred to as the "man of lawlessness" (II Thessalonians 2:3).

SIN IS TREACHERY

The word *treachery* denotes a *deceitful and unfaithful act against another*. Throughout the Scriptures, treachery is seen as an aspect belonging to all sin (Ezekiel 18:24), whether it be in rebellion (Isaiah 48:8), in forsaking the true God for idols (I Chronicles 5:25), or in any form of apostasy or turning away from God (Psalm 78:57). All sin is a betrayal of the One who created us and lovingly sustains our lives.

SIN IS AN ABOMINATION

If only one thing could be said about sin, it should be said that above all things sin is an abomination to God. An abomination before the Lord is a foul, disgusting thing. It is detestable and loathsome to God and an object of His hatred (Proverbs 6:16). In the Scriptures, all sin is an abomination and to sin is to act abominably (Ezekiel 16:52). Proverbs 28:9 declares that "He who turns away his ear from listening to the law, Even his prayer is an abomination." Similarly, Proverbs 15:8-9 declares that "The *sacrifice* of the wicked is an abomination to the Lord" and that "The *way* of the wicked is an abomination to the Lord." All idolatry (Deuteronomy 7:25) and any unjust act (Deuteronomy 25:16) is an abomination before the Lord, as well as any person who is devious (Proverbs 3:32; 15:26), a liar (Proverbs 12:22), perverse in heart (Proverbs 11:20), or proud in heart (Proverbs 16:5). In Revelation 21:8, 27, the Scriptures conclude with the warning that the abominable and those who practice abominations will suffer eternal punishment.

SIN IS MISSING THE MARK

The most common Hebrew word for *sin* is *chata*, which means *miss the mark, miss the way*, or *go wrong*. In Judges 20:16, we read that the men of Benjamin could "sling a stone at a hair and not miss [*chata*]," and in Proverbs 19:2 we read, "He who hurries his footsteps errs" or "misses the way [*chata*]." In the New Testament, the most common Greek word for *sin* is *hamartano*, which may also be translated *miss the mark, err, be mistaken*, or *wander from the path*. According to the Scriptures, the mark or goal toward which man is to aim is the glory of God (Romans 3:23). Any thought, word, or deed that does not have the glory of God as its chief end is sin. It is important to note that sin [*chata* or *hamartano*] is never seen as an innocent mistake or honest error, rather it is always a willful act of disobedience resulting from man's moral corruption and rebellion against God.

SIN IS TRESPASSING THE BOUNDARY

The word *transgress* is translated from the Hebrew word *abar* which means *cross, pass over, pass through*, or *bypass*. To transgress God's command is to go beyond what is permitted by God's commands. It is to ignore the restrictions imposed upon us by God's law and to run beyond its fence. In the New Testament, the word *transgress* is translated from the Greek word *parabaino*, which means *go by the side of, go past, pass over*, or *step over*. In Matthew 15:2-3 is found an excellent example of *parabaino*: The Pharisees asked Jesus, "Why do your disciples break [*parabaino*] the tradition of the elders? For they do not wash their hands when they eat bread." And Jesus answered them, "Why do you yourselves transgress [*parabaino*] the commandment of God for the sake of your tradition?"

THE UNIVERSALITY OF SIN

Now that we have seen something of the *sinfulness of sin*, we must turn our attention to one of the most important doctrines in all the Scriptures— *the universality of sin*. Sin is not a rare or unusual phenomenon confined to a small minority of the human race, but it is universal in scope. The Scriptures are clear that "all have sinned and fall short of the glory of God" (Romans 3:23). There is not one member of Adam's race that has not joined him in the rebellion he began. Those who would deny such a truth must deny the testimony of Scripture, of human history, and of their own sinful thoughts, words, and deeds.

1. In **Romans 3:23** is found one of the most important passages in all the Scriptures with regard to the sinfulness and disobedience of all men. What does this passage teach us?

_____

_____

_____

_____

_____

> **Note:** The phrase "fall short of the glory of God" is probably a reference to man's constant failure to do all things for God's praise, honor, and good pleasure. "For even though they knew God, they did not honor Him as God…" (Romans 1:21).

2. The Scriptures are filled with innumerable references to the sinfulness and willing disobedience of man against God and His will. What do the following Scriptures teach us about the universal disobedience of all men?

I Kings 8:46

_____

_____

_____

_____

Psalm 143:2

_____

_____

_____

_____

Proverbs 20:9

_____

_____

_____

_____

Ecclesiastes 7:20

Isaiah 53:6

3. In **Romans 3:9-12** is found a collection of Old Testament quotes ordered by the apostle Paul to demonstrate humanity's universal sinfulness and willing disobedience against God. Read the text several times until you are familiar with its contents. Then write your thoughts on each verse:

    a. *"What then? Are we better than they? Not at all; for we have already charged that both Jews and Greeks are all under sin…" (v. 9):*

    b. *" 'as it is written, 'there is none righteous, not even one…' ' " (v. 10):*

    c. *" '… There is none who understands, There is none who seeks for God…' " (v. 11):*

d. " '... all have turned aside, together they have become useless...' " (v. 12):

e. " '... There is none who does good, There is not even one.' " (v. 12):

4. The Scripture's testimony against all men is offensive, and some will not want to accept it as true. What warning is given in **I John 1:8-10** to those who would oppose the biblical testimony against man and declare that they are not sinners?

"BUT THEY REBELLED AND GRIEVED HIS HOLY SPIRIT;
THEREFORE HE TURNED HIMSELF TO BECOME THEIR ENEMY,
HE FOUGHT AGAINST THEM."

– ISAIAH 63:10 –

"GOD IS A RIGHTEOUS JUDGE,
AND A GOD WHO HAS INDIGNATION EVERY DAY."

– PSALM 7:11 –

GOD'S DISPOSITION TOWARD THE SINNER

– PART ONE –

The Scriptures teach that God is the Holy and Righteous Judge of His creation. Although He is compassionate, gracious, slow to anger, and abounding in lovingkindness, He will by no means leave the guilty unpunished (Exodus 34:6-7). When the holiness, righteousness, and love of God are confronted with the depravity and open rebellion of man, the result is divine judgment.

The writer of Ecclesiastes declared, "Behold, I have found only this, that God made men upright, but they have sought out many devices" (Ecclesiastes 7:29). This change in man must inevitably result in a change in God's disposition toward man. Man was created *upright* and was a source of great satisfaction to God. This satisfaction is seen in God's declaration that His creature man was "very good" (Genesis 1:31) and in the many blessings that He conferred upon him (Genesis 1:26-30). With the advent of sin, God's disposition was changed, joy turned to grief, satisfaction turned to anger, favor turned to hatred, and peace turned to enmity.

As we examine the disposition of God toward the sinner, we will look at passages from both the Old Testament and the New Testament. This is because many Christians are under the mistaken impression that God's disposition toward sinful man changed when Christ came into the world. They think that God was wrathful, hateful, and judgmental in the Old Testament, but that He stopped being this way when Christ was born. This is an unbiblical view of God's relationship to sinful humanity, and the only way to prove this is to show that God's disposition is consistent throughout both Testaments of Scripture.

GRIEF

Can an all-sufficient and all-powerful God suffer or experience grief? While we must affirm that the God of the Scriptures is self-determining (*i.e.* His disposition and actions are not governed by the disposition and actions of others) and immutable in His perfections (*i.e.* His nature does not change), we must equally hold to the truth that He is not apathetic or unmoved by His creature's response to Him. He is three real Persons, all of whom feel, love, hate, grieve, and are capable of entering into personal relationships.

When the Scriptures speak about God's grief, it is always in the context of man's sin. God grieves over the sin and rebellion of His creatures. This grief is the result of the offensiveness of sin to His holiness and of the destruction, misery, and loss that it brings upon His creation.

1. In **Genesis 6:6**, we find one of the Scriptures' greatest teachings regarding God's reaction to the sinfulness and rebellion of His creatures. Write your thoughts on this passage of Scripture. What does it teach us about God's disposition toward the sinner?

2. There are three other very important passages in the Old Testament that refer to God grieving over the sins of men. Write your thoughts on these passages of Scripture. What do they teach us about this very important subject?

Psalm 78:40

Isaiah 63:10

Ezekiel 6:9

3. In the New Testament, **Ephesians 4:30** is an important text regarding God's grief over man's sinfulness and rebellion against Him. What does it teach us?

4. It is important for us to understand that sin is portrayed in Scripture, not only as a thing that grieves God, but also as something that is a burden to Him. What do the following Scriptures teach us about this truth?

Isaiah 43:24

> **Note:** It is important to understand that God is not weakened by our sin, nor is His power diminished. Figurative language is being used to illustrate how the sins of man grieve the heart of God.

WRATH OR ANGER

When the holiness, justice, and love of God meet the depravity, injustice, and lovelessness of man, the inevitable result is divine anger and indignation, or the wrath of God. The word translated *wrath* in the Old Testament comes from three Hebrew words: *qetsep* (wrath, anger, indignation); *hema* (wrath, anger, disgust, displeasure, fury, rage, heat, poison); and *'aph* which literally means nostril or nose. The word came to denote anger in that the flaring of the nostrils is a sign of anger. In the New Testament, the word *wrath* is translated from two Greek words, *orge* (wrath, anger) and *thumos* (anger, indignation, passion, rage, wrath). In the Scriptures, divine wrath refers to God's holy displeasure and righteous indignation directed toward the sinner and his sin.

In speaking of the wrath of God, it is important to understand that His wrath is not an uncontrollable, irrational, or selfish emotion, but it is both the result of His holiness, righteousness, and love and also a necessary element of His government. Because of *who God is*, He must react *adversely* to sin. *God is holy*, therefore He is repulsed by evil and breaks fellowship with the wicked. *God is love* and zealously loves all that is good. Such intense love for righteousness manifests itself in an equally intense hatred of all that is evil. *God is righteous*, therefore He must judge wickedness and condemn it. In His holiness, righteousness, and love, God hates sin and comes with terrible and often violent wrath against it. If man is an object of God's wrath, it is because he has chosen to challenge God's sovereignty, has violated His holy will, has become a fountain of sin, and has exposed himself to judgment.

Today, many reject the doctrine of divine wrath or any similar teaching that would even suggest that a loving, merciful God could be wrathful or that He would manifest such wrath in the judgment and condemnation of the sinner. They argue that such ideas are nothing more than the erroneous conclusions of primitive men who saw God as hostile, vengeful, and even cruel. As Christians, we should reject any doctrine that would portray God as cruel or ignore His compassion. Nevertheless, we must not forsake the Scriptures' clear teaching on the doctrine of divine wrath and punishment—there are more references in the Scriptures with regard to the anger and wrath of God than there are to His love, kindness, and compassion. God is compassionate and gracious, slow to anger, and abounding in lovingkindness, and yet He will punish the unrepentant sinner with a view to administering justice among His creatures and vindicating His holy Name.

1. Before we proceed any further in our study of the wrath of God, it is extremely important that we understand the holy and righteous nature of God's wrath. Though man's wrath is often the result of sinful passions, the wrath of God is a manifestation of His righteousness and holiness.

    a. *According to **Romans 1:18**, why does the wrath of God fall upon man?*

    b. *According to **Exodus 15:7**, what attribute of God is revealed in every manifestation of God's wrath?*

2. How is God described in the following phrases taken from **Nahum 1:2**? Write your thoughts about these descriptions. What do they communicate to us about God?

    a. *The Lord is avenging and W_____.*

b. *The Lord reserves W_____ for His E_____.*

3. It is important to understand that the description of God as avenging and wrathful is not confined to the Old Testament. How is God described in the following Scriptures from the New Testament? Explain the meaning of these descriptions.

   a. *The God who I_____ W_____ (Romans 3:5).*

   b. *The God who is a C_____ F_____ (Hebrews 12:29)*

4. Throughout the Scriptures, several different terms are used to describe the wrath of God. It is necessary for us to consider the meaning of these terms so that we might have a better understanding of divine wrath.

   a. *According to the Scriptures given, identify the terms that are used to describe the wrath of God.*

      i.   B_____ A_____ (**Exodus 15:7**)

      ii. H_____ D_____ (**Deuteronomy 9:19**)

      iii. I_____ (**Psalm 7:11**)

      iv. F_____ (**Psalm 90:11**)

v. The F_____ A_____ of the Lord (**Jeremiah 30:24**)

b. *Explain in your own words what these terms communicate to us about the wrath of God.*

_____

_____

_____

_____

5. Throughout the Scriptures, many metaphors are employed to communicate the fierce nature of God's wrath against the sinner and his sin. In the following, we will consider a few of the most important.

a. *According to the Scriptures given, identify the metaphors that are used to describe the wrath of God.*

   i. A F_____ that Consumes (**Deuteronomy 32:22**)

   ii. A Sharpened S_____ (**Psalm 7:12**)

   iii. An A_____ of Fiery Shaft (**Psalm 7:12-13**)

   iv. A S_____ T_____ (**Jeremiah 30:23**)

   v. An O_____ F_____ (**Nahum 1:8**)

   vi. A G_____ Wine P_____ (**Revelation 14:19-20; Isaiah 63:1-6**)

b. *Explain in your own words what these metaphors communicate to us about the wrath of God.*

_____

_____

_____

_____

6. **Psalm 7:11-13** contains a very revealing description of the wrath of God as it is manifest against sin. Read the text several times until you are familiar with its contents and then write your thoughts. What does this text teach us about the wrath of God?

_____

_____

7. According to the Scriptures, the wrath of God is so intense that no man or nation is able to endure it. It can be neither overcome nor resisted. What do the following Scriptures teach us about this truth?

Jeremiah 10:10

Jeremiah 23:19-20

Nahum 1:6

8. The Scriptures also teach us that the wrath of God is so intense that it cannot be fully measured or comprehended by man. What does **Psalm 90:11** teach us about this truth?

9. As we have already stated, it is important to understand that the wrath of God is not limited to the Old Testament Scriptures, but is also clearly presented in many Scriptures of the New Testament. What do the following New Testament Scriptures teach us about the wrath of God?

Romans 1:18

Romans 2:5-6

Ephesians 2:3

Ephesians 5:3-6; Colossians 3:5-6

10. It is clear from the Scriptures that God is not only a God of love and mercy, but of wrath and vengeance. In His holiness, righteousness, and love, God hates sin and comes with terrible and often violent vengeance against it. If man challenges God's sovereignty and violates His will, then he will expose himself to His wrath. According to the following Scriptures, how should all men respond to this truth?

Psalm 76:7

Psalm 90:11-12

_____

_____

_____

_____

11. Even though the reality of the wrath of God is undeniable, we should also understand that He is merciful. God takes no pleasure in the death of the wicked (Ezekiel 18:23), but will delay His wrath and give the sinner ample opportunity to turn away from his sin. Nevertheless, those who continue in rebellion will most certainly face the wrath of God. What do the following Scriptures teach us about this truth?

Exodus 34:6-7

_____

_____

_____

_____

Nahum 1:3

_____

_____

_____

_____

"For You are not a God who takes pleasure in wickedness; No evil dwells with You. The boastful shall not stand before Your eyes; You hate all who do iniquity."

– Psalm 5:4-5 –

"They profess to know God, but by their deeds they deny Him, being detestable and disobedient and worthless for any good deed."

– Titus 1:16 –

GOD'S DISPOSITION TOWARD THE SINNER

– PART TWO –

HATRED

Closely related to the wrath or anger of God is His hatred. Words that are often used in association with God's hatred are abhor, detest, loathe, etc. Many object to any teaching about the hatred of God on the false assumption that God *cannot* hate because "God is love" (I John 4:8). While the love of God is a reality that goes beyond comprehension, it is important to see that the love of God is the very reason for His hatred. We should not say, "God is love, and therefore He *cannot* hate," but rather, "God is love, and therefore He *must* hate." If a person truly *loves* life, acknowledges it sanctity, and cherishes all children as a gift from God, then they must *hate* abortion. It is impossible to passionately and purely love children and yet be neutral toward that which destroys them in the womb. In the same way, if God loves *with the greatest intensity* all that is upright and good, then He must *with equal intensity* hate all that is perverse and evil.

The Scriptures teach us that God not only hates sin, but that His hatred is directed toward those who practice sin. We have been taught that God loves the sinner and hates the sin, but such teaching is a denial of the Scriptures that clearly declare that God not only hates *iniquity*, but that He hates *"all who do iniquity"* (Psalm 5:5). We must understand that it is impossible to separate the sin from the sinner. God does not punish *sin*, but He punishes the *sinner*. It is not sin that is condemned to hell, but the man who practices it.

What does it mean when the Scriptures declare that God hates sinners? The following should be considered: *First*, Webster defines *hate* as a feeling of extreme enmity toward someone, to regard another with active hostility, or to have a strong aversion toward another: to detest, loathe, abhor, or abominate. Although these are hard words, most, if not all, are used in the Scripture to describe God's relationship to sin and the sinner. *Secondly*, we must understand that God's hatred exists in perfect harmony with His other attributes. Unlike man, God's hatred is never the result of some weakness or defect in His character—there are none. Rather, God's hatred is holy, just, and a result of His love. *Thirdly*, we must understand that God's hatred is not a denial of His love. Psalm 5:5 is not a denial of John 3:16 or Matthew 5:44-45. Although God's wrath abides upon the sinner, although He is angry with the wicked every day, and although He hates all who do iniquity, His love is of such a nature that He is able to love those who are the very objects of His hatred and work on their behalf for their salvation. *Fourthly*, although God is longsuffering toward the objects of His hatred and holds out to them the offer of salvation, there will come a time when He will withdraw His offer, and reconciliation will no longer be possible. Sinful men should consider this truth with fear and trembling.

1. The Scriptures clearly teach that God not only hates the sin, but that His hatred is directed toward those who practice sin. What does **Psalm 5:4-5** teach us about this truth?

2. Psalm 5:5 is not alone in attesting to the holy hatred of God against sin and those who do wrong. In **Psalm 11:4-7** is found another very important text concerning God's hatred. What does this text teach us? Write your thoughts on each of the following phrases:

a. *"The Lord is in His holy temple; the Lord's throne is in heaven..." (v. 4):*

b. *"... His eyes behold, His eyelids test the sons of men. The Lord tests the righteous and the wicked... (vs. 4-5):*

c. *"... And the one who loves violence His soul hates." (v. 5):*

d. *"Upon the wicked He will rain snares; Fire and brimstone and burning wind will be the portion of their cup." (v. 6):*

e. *"For the Lord is righteous, He loves righteousness; The upright will behold His face." (v. 7):*

_____

_____

_____

_____

3. In the following, we will consider six passages of Scripture that employ the words abhor, detest, loathe, and abomination. Our purpose is to understand, in greater depths, God's holy hatred toward sin and the sinner. Carefully read each text and write your comments. What do they teach us?

Leviticus 20:23

_____

_____

_____

_____

Deuteronomy 18:12; 25:16

_____

_____

_____

_____

Psalm 95:10

_____

_____

_____

_____

Titus 1:16

_____

_____

_____

Revelation 21:8

ENMITY

We often hear about sinful man's unceasing war against God, but little is taught about God's unceasing war against the wicked. The hostility between God and the sinner is not one-sided, but mutual. The Scriptures clearly teach that God considers the sinner to be His enemy and has declared war upon him. The sinner's only hope is to drop his weapon and lift the white flag of surrender before it is forever too late. This is the clear teaching of Scripture.

1. In **Nahum 1:2** is found a reference to the enmity that God has toward the sinner and the judgment that follows. Read the text and write your thoughts on the following phrases.

   a. *"The Lord takes vengeance on His adversaries…"*

   b. *"… And He reserves wrath for His enemies."*

2. Another important Old Testament reference to the enmity of God against the sinner is found in **Isaiah 63:10**. This Scripture not only demonstrates the enmity of God against the sinner, but also reveals the reason for such enmity. Read the text and write your thoughts.

_____

_____

_____

_____

3. In **Romans 5:10** is found one of the most important references in the Scriptures with regard to the enmity of God against the sinner. It also demonstrates that this doctrine is not limited to the Old Testament, but reaches into the New. Write your thoughts on this passage.

_____

_____

_____

_____

Note: It is often held that man is the enemy of God, but God is never the enemy of man. However, this statement is quite misleading. In Romans 5:10, both ideas are present, but the reader should keep in mind that the sinner's opposition to God is only secondary. The primary thought of the text is God's holy opposition to the sinner.

VENGEANCE

Closely related to the wrath of God is His vengeance. In the Scriptures, the desire for vengeance is often presented as a vice of wicked men (Leviticus 19:18; I Samuel 25:25, 30-33). Therefore, it is difficult for us to understand how a holy and loving God could be a _God of Vengeance_. What we must understand is that God's vengeance is always motivated by His zeal for holiness and justice.

Today, many reject the doctrine of divine vengeance or any teaching that would even suggest that a loving and merciful God could be vengeful. They would argue that such ideas are nothing more than the erroneous conclusions of primitive men who saw God as hostile and cruel. As Christians, we should reject any doctrine that would portray God as cruel or ignore His compassion. Nevertheless, we must not forsake the Scripture's clear teaching on the doctrine of divine vengeance. God is compassionate and gracious, slow to anger, and abounding in lovingkindness, but He is also just. He will punish the sinner with the purpose of vindicating His Name and administering justice among His creatures. In light of man's sin, God is right to avenge Himself. Three times in the book of Jeremiah, God asks, "Shall I not punish them for these things? On a nation such as this shall I not avenge Myself?" (5:9, 29; 9:9).

1. In the Scriptures, a name often carries great significance and communicates something about the one who bears it. What does the divine name in **Psalm 94:1** reveal to us about God?

2. How is God described in **Nahum 1:2**? Explain the meaning of these descriptions. What do they communicate to us about God?

   a. *A J_____ and A_____ God is the Lord.*

   b. *The Lord takes V_____ on His A_____.*

3. In **Deuteronomy 32:39-42** is found one of the most terrifying illustrations of God's vengeance against those who despise His authority and violate His law. Read the passage carefully and write your thoughts on each phrase.

a. *"See now that I, I am He, and there is no god besides Me..." (v. 39):*

b. *"... It is I who put to death and give life. I have wounded and it is I who heal, And there is no one who can deliver from My hand." (v. 39):*

c. *"If I sharpen My flashing sword, And My hand takes hold on justice, I will render vengeance on My adversaries, And I will repay those who hate Me." (v. 41):*

d. *"I will make My arrows drunk with blood, And My sword will devour flesh, with the blood of the slain and the captives..." (v. 42):*

4. Before we turn our attention to the New Testament, we will consider two more Old Testament Scriptures that give greater insight into the reality and meaning of God's vengeance against the sinner and his sin. Write your thoughts.

Deuteronomy 7:9-10

Isaiah 1:24

5. It is important to understand that the doctrine of divine vengeance is not limited to the Old Testament, but is clearly taught in the New Testament. Whenever the holiness, justice, and love of God are confronted with man's rebellion, the result is divine wrath and vengeance. What do the following Scriptures teach us about this truth?

   Romans 12:19

   I Thessalonians 4:1-6

   Hebrews 10:30-31

"FOR THE WRATH OF GOD IS REVEALED FROM HEAVEN AGAINST ALL UNGODLINESS AND UNRIGHTEOUSNESS OF MEN WHO SUPPRESS THE TRUTH IN UNRIGHTEOUSNESS, BECAUSE THAT WHICH IS KNOWN ABOUT GOD IS EVIDENT WITHIN THEM; FOR GOD MADE IT EVIDENT TO THEM."

– ROMANS 1:18-19 –

GOD'S JUDGMENT UPON THE SINNER

Having considered God's disposition toward the unrepentant sinner, we will now consider the actual judgments that result from sin. There are many today who *avoid* the doctrine of divine judgment and others who *deny* it altogether. However, if we believe the Scripture to be the inspired Word of God, we must accept this doctrine with the same conviction as the rest. God is the Judge of all the earth (Genesis 18:25) who will punish the wicked according to what is due them.

SEPARATED FROM GOD

God is morally perfect and separated from all evil. It is impossible for Him to take pleasure in sin or join in fellowship with those who practice unrighteousness. Therefore, man's moral corruption and unrighteousness stand as a great wall between himself and God and make fellowship with God impossible. Unless this sin is taken out of the way, man is destined to live and die outside of God's fellowship, cut off from the fullness of His blessing.

1. In His holiness, God cannot be neutral about sin or those who practice it, but must hate sin and turn away from it as an abomination. What does **Habakkuk 1:13** teach us about this truth?

_____

_____

_____

_____

_____

2. The Scriptures not only teach us that sin is repugnant to God, but that it results in broken fellowship between God and the sinner. What do the following Scriptures teach about this truth?

    Proverbs 15:29

_____

_____

_____

_____

    Isaiah 59:1-2

_____

_____

_____

_____

3. In the book of Ephesians, we find several texts that describe the great separation that existed between the pagan gentiles and the one true God. These texts also illustrate the great separation that exists between God and the sinner. According to the following Scriptures, how is the sinner described?

    a. *S_____ from Christ (Ephesians 2:12)*

    b. *E_____ from the commonwealth (i.e. citizenship) among God's people (Ephesians 2:12)*

    c. *A S_____ to the covenants of promise (Ephesians 2:12)*

    d. *Having no H_____ (Ephesians 2:12)*

e. *And without G_____ in the world* **(Ephesians 2:12)**

f. *A S_____ and A_____* **(Ephesians 2:19)**

g. *E_____ from the life of God* **(Ephesians 4:18)**

4. Based upon the Scriptures we have studied in questions 1-3, explain how man's sin results in broken fellowship and separation from God:

GIVEN OVER TO SIN

The Scriptures teach that all men are born spiritually dead and morally depraved, and that they possess an almost limitless capacity for evil. If they were allowed to give full rein to their depravity, the result would be the abolition of man. For the preservation of society and for His own purpose and glory, God restrains the wickedness of men and keeps them from being the worst that they could be. This restraining work of God is the only thing that stands between an on-going humanity and self-annihilation. It is one of the greatest manifestations of God's grace toward all.

The divine act of 'giving men over' to their sin occurs when God ceases to restrain man's evil or allows man more freedom to exercise his depravity. God withdraws His restraining grace and turns men over to the moral corruption and depravity of their own hearts. It leads to destruction and is one of the most terrible manifestations of the wrath of God. In the following, we will consider one of the darkest texts in all the Word of God—**Romans 1:18-32**. The most terrifying thing about this passage is that the judgment of which it speaks has been manifested in differing degrees in every generation since the fall, including our own. Read Romans 1:18-32 several times until you are familiar with its contents and then answer the following questions.

1. According to verse 18, against whom is the wrath of God revealed and why?

2. According to verses 19-20, how is it that the Scriptures can rightly declare that all men are *"without excuse,"* even those who have never had the privilege of the written revelation of God through the Scriptures?

Note: This does not mean that all men know everything that may be known about God or that all men are granted the same degree of revelation. It means that all men, everywhere and at all times, possess sufficient knowledge of the one true God so that they will be without excuse for their sins on the Day of Judgment. Although limited, God's revelation of Himself to all men has not been ambiguous or unclear. He has made it "evident" to all men that there is one true God and that He alone should be worshipped. The phrase "within them" proves that the knowledge of the one true God is not only demonstrated through the works of creation, but that God Himself has imprinted this knowledge upon the very heart of every man. The universe which God has made and which proves His existence simply acts as a confirmation or reminder of what all men already know—there is one true God who is worthy of worship and obedience.

3. According to verses 21-25, what has been the universal response of mankind to the revelation of God?

   a. *"For even though they knew God, they did not honor Him as God or give thanks…"* (v. 21):

   b. *"… but they became futile in their speculations, and their foolish heart was darkened."* (v. 21):

c. *"Professing to be wise, they became fools..." (v. 22):*

d. *"... and exchanged the glory of the incorruptible God for an image in the form of corruptible man and of birds and four-footed animals and crawling creatures." (v. 23):*

e. *"For they exchanged the truth of God for a lie, and worshiped and served the creature rather than the Creator, who is blessed forever. Amen." (v. 25):*

4. In verse 18, we learned that the wrath of God is revealed from heaven against men who willingly deny and suppress the truth. According to verses 24, 26, and 28, how is the wrath of God manifested against them?

GIVEN OVER TO MISERIES

The sin to which men are given over leads to innumerable and indescribable temporal miseries. Except for the reality of death, the miseries of this present life are possibly the greatest evidence of God's judgment upon sin. We are not only fallen creatures, but also we live in a fallen world. Our existence is not only fleeting, but also encumbered with great difficulties and hardships. There are miseries from without and within.

There is a tendency in our present age of Christianity to explain away these miseries of life as 'natural' consequences of sin and deny any possibility that they might be the result of God's sovereign justice and wrath. Many seek to remove any responsibility from God and somehow protect Him from accusations of lovelessness or cruelty. Nevertheless, the Scriptures clearly reveal that the temporal miseries of this life are, in varying degrees, a result of God's judgment upon the sinner and the fallen world in which he dwells. Even though not all the suffering experienced by a person is due to sins he commits (see John 9:1-3), there would still be no suffering in the world had man not sinned. Romans 1:18 teaches us that the wrath of God *is presently revealed* from heaven against the ungodliness and unrighteousness of men. Therefore, the temporal miseries of this world are one aspect of this revelation.

Although the temporal miseries that engulf every aspect of human life are primarily a revelation of God's justice and wrath, they are not void of mercy. Every misery and hardship from birth to death is also a divine reminder to man of his falleness, the corruption of his soul, and his alienation from God. The pain of childbirth calls out to man. The calamities, natural catastrophes, wars, pestilences, and famines of this world call out to man. The disappointments and frustrations of this life call out to man. The inward struggles of dissatisfaction and restlessness call out to man. The ever-present threat of death calls out to man:

"You are lost and must be found; you are alienated and must be reconciled;
you are fallen and must be raised; you are dislocated and must be set right;
you are disfigured and must be transformed."

1. **Genesis 3:16-19** contains a description of the misery that fell upon mankind and creation as a result of sin. Explain how each misery is both a revelation of God's judgment and a revelation of His mercy.

a. *The Judgment Upon the Woman (v. 16)*

_____

_____

_____

_____

b. *The Judgment Upon the Man (vs. 17-19)*

_____

_____

_____

_____

2. The consequences of the curse that have fallen upon man since the first rebellion of Adam are clearly set before us in the wisdom literature of Scripture. What do the following texts from Job, Psalms, and Ecclesiastes teach us about the inevitable miseries and frustrations of fallen man?

Job 5:7

_____

_____

_____

_____

Job 7:1-3

_____

_____

_____

_____

Psalm 89:47

_____

_____

_____

Ecclesiastes 2:22-23

"... For in the day that you eat from it you will surely die."

– Genesis 2:17 –

"For the wages of sin is death."

– Romans 6:23 –

GOD'S JUDGMENT OF DEATH

SUBJECT TO DEATH

Without a doubt, the greatest proof of the wrath of God against the unrighteousness of man is physical death—the separation of the soul from the body. From Adam until the present, all men are faced with the terrible and undeniable reality that they will die. Regardless of human greatness, power, or social position, death is the unavoidable destiny that awaits all men. The Scriptures teach us that this terrifying reality is the result of sin. It is important to note that death is not annihilation. Once born, men do not cease to exist, but will continue on either in eternal communion with God in heaven or in eternal separation from Him in hell.

Again, it is necessary that one find in death, not only divine judgment, but also mercy. Death is 'God's Great Reminder' to man of his mortality and need of redemption. Every obituary, every funeral procession, every grave marker cries out to man to turn from the concerns of this world to the concerns of eternity, to make ready for the Reaper, to prepare to meet his God.

A BIBLICAL DESCRIPTION OF DEATH

Although death is an undeniable reality that confronts mankind relentlessly, its exact nature remains a mystery to the living. We cannot rely upon even the most sincere accounts of those who have supposedly 'gone to the other side' and returned to tell us. If we are to have a 'sure word' about so great a mystery, we must turn to the Scriptures.

The Holy Scripture speaks often about death with many warnings and exhortations, and yet it offers few answers with regard to its exact nature. What can be known for sure must be gleaned from the few direct references found in the Scripture. These teach us two great truths:

- *Death is not the end of conscious human existence.*
- *At death, the body returns to the ground (until the resurrection), and the spirit returns to God.*

1. In **James 2:26** is found a simple, yet profound description of death. Meditate upon the text and then write your thoughts. What is death? When does death occur?

_____

_____

_____

_____

2. From James 2:26, we learned that the spirit is separated from the body at death. In **Ecclesiastes 12:7**, we will discover one of the most profound truths ever revealed to mortal man. According to this text, what happens to the body and the spirit at the moment of separation? (The same truth is found in **Psalm 146:4**.)

_____

_____

_____

_____

3. In the Scriptures, several important metaphors are employed to help us understand the nature of death. Identify each of the following metaphors.

   a. *To B_____ one's L_____ (Genesis 49:33)*

   b. *To P_____ away (Job 34:20)*

   c. *To R_____ to D_____ (Genesis 3:19; Psalm 104:29)*

   d. *To be C_____ off (Job 24:24)*

   e. *To D_____ (II Timothy 4:6; II Peter 1:15)*

Death as a Manifestation of God's Judgment

From its first mention in the Scriptures, death is treated as the result of God's judgment against the sinner (Genesis 2:17). Why do humans die? The Scriptures' response is clear and unapologetic—they die because they are sinners. God declared to Adam, "For in the day that you eat from it you will surely die." From this text and others, it is clear that death was not woven into the fabric of the original creation, but entered into our world through the sin of Adam and has passed on to all men, for all men sin. Every tombstone and grave marker is a manifestation of God's judgment against our fallen race. To say that death is a manifestation of God's judgment does not necessarily mean that some die sooner than others because they are greater sinners. There are children who die in the womb without committing a single act of sin, and there are those who live in open rebellion against God for decades. It simply means that every one of us is part of a fallen, sinful race, and that death is one manifestation of God's judgment against us.

1. Throughout the Scriptures, death is seen as the result of man's sin. Whether it is the imputed sin of Adam or the personal unrighteousness of all men, the principle is the same—all men die because all men sin. What do the following Scriptures from the Old and New Testaments teach us about this truth?

   Ezekiel 18:4, 20

   _____

   _____

   _____

   _____

   Romans 6:23

   _____

   _____

   _____

   _____

2. Both the Old and New Testaments are clear and unapologetic—the inevitable consequence of sin is death. In **James 1:15**, the Scriptures reveal to us the inner

workings of sin in the life of man and its fatal results. Read the text several times until you are familiar with its contents and then write your thoughts:

_____

_____

_____

_____

> **Note:** When fallen man gives in to his sinful desires, the result is sin, and the end of sin is always death.

3. In **Isaiah 64:6**, the relationship between *man's sin* and *death* is illustrated in poetic fashion. Read the text until you are familiar with its contents, and then write your answers to following questions:

   a. *How is man's moral corruption described?*

   _____

   _____

   _____

   _____

   b. *What are the inevitable consequences of man's moral corruption and active pursuit of sin?*

   _____

   _____

   _____

   _____

4. **Psalm 90:3-10** is a tremendous poetic portrayal of death as a manifestation of God's judgment against sinful men. Write your thoughts on each of the following verses.

   a. *'You turn man back into dust and say, "Return, O children of men."' (v. 3):*

   _____

   _____

   _____

   _____

b. *"You have swept them away like a flood, they fall asleep; In the morning they are like grass which sprouts anew. In the morning it flourishes and sprouts anew; Toward evening it fades and withers away." (vs. 5-6):*

c. *"For we have been consumed by Your anger and by Your wrath we have been dismayed. You have placed our iniquities before You, our secret sins in the light of Your presence. For all our days have declined in Your fury; We have finished our years like a sigh." (vs. 7-9):*

d. *"As for the days of our life, they contain seventy years, or if due to strength, eighty years, yet their pride is but labor and sorrow; For soon it is gone and we fly away." (v. 10):*

DEATH AS A SOVEREIGN DECREE AND WORK OF GOD

According to the Scriptures, death is a consequence of God's judgment against man's sin. Not only will all men die, but all will die according to the sovereign decree of God. He has not only appointed the day of our death, but He Himself will bring it about. He gives life and takes it, makes alive and kills. Much of contemporary Christian thought would be extremely hesitant to admit that death is the result of the sovereign decree and work of God. They would rather explain death as a mere consequence of living in a fallen world, or as something beyond the control of a loving Creator. This is a blatant contradiction of the testimony of Scripture.

1. How is God described in **Daniel 5:23**? Complete the description and then explain its meaning:

   a. *The God in whose H_____ are your L_____-B_____ and your W_____.*

   _____

   _____

   _____

   _____

2. The Scriptures are clear and unapologetic that God is absolutely sovereign over the life and death of every man. The following are two of the most important texts in Scripture with regard to this truth. What do they teach us?

   Deuteronomy 32:39

   _____

   _____

   _____

   _____

   I Samuel 2:6

   _____

   _____

   _____

   _____

3. The sovereignty of God teaches us that the death of every man has already been appointed by divine decree. A certain number of days have been given to us all. They will not be extended even one breath beyond what God has determined. What do the following Scriptures teach us about this truth?

   Job 14:5

   _____

   _____

   _____

   _____

Ecclesiastes 3:2

_____

_____

_____

_____

Hebrews 9:27

_____

_____

_____

_____

Luke 12:20

_____

_____

_____

_____

THE UNIVERSALITY OF DEATH

One biblical truth that stands without any opponent—whether it be in the realm of science, history, or letters—is that all men die. The great mass of humanity lives under an unrelenting mortal plague. Billions have fallen from it scourge, and everyday thousands more join the number. There is no cure, and there is no hope that it will somehow dissipate with time.

Death is so frequent and widespread that it may seem unnecessary to consider its universality. However, it is necessary to consider such a doctrine, not because it is denied, but because it is often forgotten. We know that we are mortal creatures. We know that we are dying. We know that we cannot escape death or even impede its coming. Therefore, we consciously or unconsciously seek to drive the thought of death as far from us as possible. We have become so proficient at banishing death from our thoughts that we can carry the caskets of our closest friends without one moment's meditation on the truth that the same fate awaits us all. For this reason, it is necessary for us to hear the truth we often neglect:

1. In the Scriptures, there is a very important metaphor used to communicate the universality of death. Identify this metaphor and explain it meaning.

   a. *The W_____ of all the E_____* (**Joshua 23:14; I Kings 2:1-2**)

2. **Hebrews 9:27** is possibly the most important passage in the Scriptures regarding the universality of death. What truths are revealed in this text?

3. An important truth that is often taught in the Scriptures is that death is not a respecter of persons. It comes on all men alike—rich and poor, wise and foolish. What do the following Scriptures teach us about this truth?

   Job 21:22-26

   Ecclesiastes 2:16

THE BREVITY, FRAILTY, AND FUTILITY OF MAN

The first man was created in the image of God. With the advent of sin much was lost, and man's existence became tragically twisted and deformed. Man became a being of brief duration, weariness, and futility. He lives his life until all vitality is drained away, every purpose is demolished, and the body finally returns to the dust from which it came. It is not without reason that the preacher cries out, "Vanity of vanities! All is vanity!" (Ecclesiastes 1:2).

1. Throughout the Scriptures are numerous descriptions of the frailty of man, the brevity of his life, and the futility of all his strivings. The following texts are some of the most important. Meditate upon each text, answering the following questions: What are the metaphors used to describe man and his life? What do these metaphors communicate?

Job 14:1-2

Psalm 39:4-6

Psalm 78:39

Psalm 103:14-16

Psalm 144:3-4

James 4:14

2. Within the book of Job are two passages that illustrate both the frailty and brevity of a man's life. Meditate carefully upon each text and write your thoughts:

   a. *The Frailty of a Man's Life (Job 4:18-21)*

   b. *The Brevity of a Man's Life (Job 9:25-26)*

3. In the following passages are found a few of the most striking descriptions of the futility and vanity of a man's life. Read each text until you are familiar with its contents and then write your thoughts. How is the futility of a man's life described?

Psalm 49:10-14

_____

_____

_____

_____

Ecclesiastes 3:19-20

_____

_____

_____

_____

Ecclesiastes 5:15-17

_____

_____

_____

_____

I Timothy 6:7

_____

_____

_____

_____

4. The Scriptures teach that all men sin and therefore all men die. Death is the inevitable reality that awaits every one of us. As fallen creatures, death is an enemy which we cannot avoid, escape, or defeat. What do the following passages of Scripture teach us about this truth?

Job 14:7-12

_____

_____

_____

Psalm 49:7-9

Psalm 89:48

Ecclesiastes 8:8

5. To bring our study of the frailty of man and the brevity of life to a close, we will consider two final texts of Scripture—**Isaiah 40:6-8** and **Ecclesiastes 12:1**. In the former is found one of the most majestic declarations of both the brevity of man and eternality of God. In the latter is found an extremely important admonition to perishing man. Read each text until you are familiar with its contents, and then write the truths that you have gleaned.

a. *The Truth about Man (Isaiah 40:6-8)*

b. *How then shall we live (Ecclesiastes 12:1)?*

"Do not marvel at this; for an hour is coming, in which all who are in the tombs will hear His voice, and will come forth; those who did the good deeds to a resurrection of life, those who committed the evil deeds to a resurrection of judgment."

– John 5:28-29 –

THE FINAL JUDGMENT OF THE WICKED

Possibly the most awesome doctrine in all the Scriptures is that of the final judgment. The truth that everyone of Adam's race will stand before a righteous and all-knowing God, and be judged according to their every thought, word, and deed, is something that goes beyond the scope of our wildest imaginations.

Although the doctrine of final judgment is often scorned and rejected as a relic from the past, it must be remembered that it is the clear teaching of Scripture, and a reasonable truth to accept in light of what we know about the attributes of God. It is certainly within God's prerogative to *govern* the creatures He has created as well as *judge* the creatures He governs. It is not only His prerogative, but it is demanded by His righteous character. *Shall not the judge of all the earth do right?* Is it not necessary that a moral God carry out moral justice in the universe He has made? Shall we deny God the very right we demand for ourselves in our own courts of law? Certainly not!

A FUNDAMENTAL DOCTRINE OF THE SCRIPTURES

The final judgment is a fundamental doctrine of the Scriptures. It is impossible to hold to the divine inspiration and infallibility of the Scriptures without embracing the doctrine of the final judgment and eternal condemnation of the wicked.

Although much of what we may like to know about this doctrine remains a mystery, it is an absolute certainty of Scripture. Everyone of Adam's race will be judged by God. The wicked will be condemned to eternal punishment, and the redeemed in Christ will inherit the fullness of salvation.

1. The final judgment is an essential doctrine of the Scriptures and the Christian faith. This truth is clearly communicated by the writer of **Hebrews 6:1-2** who refers to the doctrine as:

    a. *An E_____ teaching about the Christ.*

    > **Note:** The word comes from the Greek word *arche*, which means *beginning* or *origin*. It means that the doctrine of eternal judgment is a basic or foundational teaching of Christianity. It is not a theological speculation, but a biblical certainty.

2. God's final judgment of mankind is so embedded in Old Testament thought that to deny the reality of the coming judgment would be to deny the infallibility of the Scriptures. What do the following Old Testament Scriptures teach us about the certainty of God's final judgment?

    Psalm 9:7-8

    _____

    _____

    _____

    _____

    Psalm 96:10-13

    _____

    _____

    _____

    _____

    Ecclesiastes 3:17

    _____

    _____

Ecclesiastes 11:9

Ecclesiastes 12:13-14

3. It is important to understand that the doctrine of eternal judgment is not only an 'Old Testament doctrine', as some might claim. What do the following New Testament Scriptures teach us about the certainty of God's final judgment?

John 5:28-29

Romans 14:10-12

Hebrews 9:27

II Peter 3:7

_____

_____

_____

_____

Revelation 20:12

_____

_____

_____

_____

4. In the Scriptures, there are many names given to describe that *day* when God will judge all men. Identify each name according to the text listed and then write your thoughts on what each name communicates to us.

a. *The D____ of J_____ (II Peter 2:9)*

_____

_____

_____

b. *The day of W_____ and revelation of the righteous J_____ of God* **(Romans 2:5)**

_____

_____

_____

c. *The G_____ D____ (Jude 6)*

_____

_____

d. *The D____ of G____ (II Peter 3:12)*

5. On the day of judgment, God will consider the thoughts, words, and deeds of every member of Adam's race. What do the following Scriptures teach us about the thoroughness of God's judgment? Will anything be overlooked or hidden before Him?

Luke 12:2-3

Ecclesiastes 12:14

I Corinthians 4:5

Hebrews 4:13

6. **Revelation 20:11-15** is the most descriptive passage in the Scriptures regarding the final judgment. Read the text several times until you are familiar with its contents and then answer the following questions:

a. *How are God and the throne of God described in verse 11? How are the greatness and awesomeness of God communicated?*

b. *According to verses 12-13, who are standing before the throne of God? Does anyone escape from the judgment or is anyone exempt? Explain your answer.*

c. *According to verses 12-13, how are men judged? What is the basis for God's judgment? Is the judgment thorough? Explain your answer.*

d. *According to verses 14-15, what is the fate of everyone who has rejected Jesus Christ and are judged according their own deeds?*

"I say to you, My friends, do not be afraid of those who kill the body and after that have no more that they can do. But I will warn you whom to fear: fear the One who, after He has killed, has authority to cast into hell; yes, I tell you, fear Him!"

– Luke 12:4-5 –

"For God so loved the world, that He gave His only begotten Son, that whoever believes in Him shall not perish, but have eternal life."

– John 3:16 –

HELL

We have learned that the wrath of God is manifested against humanity in man's alienation from God, his being turned over to sin, his exposure to misery, and his subjection to physical death. In this lesson, we will consider the greatest of all manifestations of divine wrath—*hell*. One of the most solemn truths of Scripture is that the consequences of sin do not end with physical death. After death, there is a final judgment, and those who die in their sins will spend eternity in hell. Even though this doctrine is often ridiculed and rejected, we cannot ignore the clear teaching of Scripture—there is a place of eternal judgment for the wicked.

HADES AND GEHENNA

In the New Testament, two specific terms are used with reference to hell—*Hades and Gehenna*. We can come to a clearer understanding of the nature of hell through a careful study of these two references.

HADES

The word *Hades* comes from the Greek word *hades,* which occurs ten times in the New Testament (Matthew 11:23; 16:18; Luke 10:15; 16:23; Acts 2:27, 31; Revelation 1:18; 6:8; 20:13-14). Although it is most often employed as a reference to death and the general abode of the dead, it is clearly used in Luke 16:23 with reference to a place where the wicked are tormented. There are two major interpretations with regard to Hades and its relationship to Gehenna: (1) Hades and Gehenna refer to the same place of torment. Before the resurrection and the last judgment, the wicked suffer in a disembodied state. After the resurrection and the last judgment, the wicked are united with their resurrected bodies and returned to the same place of torment. (2) Hades is the temporary abode of the disembodied wicked until the resurrection and the last judgment, when the wicked are reunited with their bodies and assigned to an eternal place of torment called Gehenna. This second interpretation seems more likely, given that Hades will someday be destroyed (Revelation 20:14) while the suffering in Gehenna is unending (Mark 9:47-48).

GEHENNA

The word *Gehenna* occurs twelve times in the New Testament (Matthew 5:22, 29-30; 10:28; 18:9; 23:15, 33; Mark 9:43, 47; Luke 12:5; James 3:6). It is the Greek form of the Aramaic expression *gehinnam*, which refers to the *valley of Hinnom* (Joshua 15:8), located to the south of Jerusalem (today it is called *Wadi er-Rababi*). Under the reigns of the wicked kings Ahaz and Manasseh, it was a place where parents offered their children as sacrifices to the Ammonite god Molech (see Jeremiah 32:35; II Kings 16:3; 21:6). During the reign of Josiah, the practice of child sacrifice was ended and the valley of Hinnom was desecrated (II Kings 23:10-14). It eventually became a refuse pile for garbage, the carcasses of dead animals, and the bodies of executed criminals. It was a place of continuous fire and smoke and was infested with maggots, worms, and vermin. By the time of Christ, the word *Gehenna* was commonly employed to denote the place of final punishment and torment for the wicked—*a place of eternal death, pollution, defilement, and misery.*

THE NATURE OF HELL

In any attempt to understand the nature of hell, we must proceed with much caution. On one hand, we must be careful to follow the Scriptures and not the fanciful descriptions of hell created by both ancient and modern literature and media. On the other hand, we must be careful not to explain away the doctrine of hell or diminish its horrors. According to the Scriptures, and especially the teachings of Jesus Christ, there is a real place called hell that is both terrible in its suffering and eternal in it duration.

Exclusion from the Favorable Presence of God

The first, and possibly the most terrible, aspect of hell is exclusion from the favorable presence of God. In modern Evangelical thinking, hell is often described as a place of torment outside of the presence of God. It is often said that heaven is heaven because of the presence of God, and hell is hell because of His absence. Although this statement has an element of truth, it is extremely misleading. It is not the absence of God that makes hell a place of torment, but the absence of His favorable presence. In fact, hell is hell because *God is there in the fullness of His justice and wrath.*

1. **II Thessalonians 1:9-10** is one of the most important texts in Scripture with regard to the separation of the wicked from the favorable presence of God. Read the text until you are familiar with its contents and then write your thoughts.

2. In the Scriptures, several texts refer to the final judgment and hell as being cast out or excluded from the presence of God. Consider each text carefully and then write your thoughts.

   Matthew 7:23; Luke 13:27

   Matthew 8:11-12; 22:13; 25:30

3. It is not the absence of *God* that makes hell a place of torment, but the absence of *His favorable presence*. Without taking anything away from the texts we just considered, it is important to note that hell is hell because God is there in *the fullness of His justice and wrath*. What do the following texts teach us about this truth?

Revelation 14:9-10

_____

_____

_____

_____

Isaiah 30:33

_____

_____

_____

_____

INDESCRIBABLE SUFFERING

It is impossible to be faithful to the Scriptures, especially to the words of Jesus, while at the same time seeking to deny or ignore the truths that they teach regarding the suffering of the wicked in hell. As we will see, the Scriptures, and especially Jesus, speak about hell has a place of indescribable suffering. It is rightly said that the bliss of heaven goes beyond the mind to comprehend and the power of human language to communicate. According to the Scriptures, the same may be said of the sufferings and terrors of hell. It is important to remember that although the doctrine of hell is repulsive to many, it does not make it any less a reality.

Before we proceed, it is important to understand that hell is not a place where the wicked are cruelly tortured, but where they suffer perfect justice for their sin. God is not cruel. He does not gleefully torture His enemies. In fact, the Bible teaches that God takes no pleasure in the death of the wicked (Ezekiel 18:23, 32). God is a God of justice, and hell is the place where that justice is dispensed. The wicked receive the exact measure of punishment that is due them.

1. According to the words of Jesus in the following Scriptures, how is hell described? What does each description teach us about the suffering found in hell?

   a. *A place of T_____ (Luke 16:28)*

   _____

   _____

   _____

   _____

   b. *A place where there is W_____ and G_____ of teeth (Matthew 8:12)*

   _____

   _____

   _____

   _____

   Note: This description of the sufferings of the wicked in hell is important because of its frequent use by Jesus (Matthew 13:42, 50; 22:13; 24:51; 25:30; Luke 13:28).

2. The following two passages of Scripture reveal to us something of the indescribable suffering of hell. Read through each passage until you are familiar with its contents and then summarize what is revealed to us about the torments of hell.

   Luke 16:19-31

   _____

   _____

   _____

   Revelation 14:9-11

   _____

   _____

   _____

   _____

3. Although the Bible makes it clear that *every inhabitant* in hell will suffer unspeakable torment, it also teaches that this suffering will be *according to the sinfulness of each person's life*. What do the following Scriptures teach us about this truth?

Matthew 11:20-24

_____

_____

_____

_____

Luke 12:42-48

_____

_____

_____

_____

Matthew 23:14

_____

_____

_____

_____

UNENDING PUNISHMENT

Possibly the most frightful truth about hell is that it is eternal. All who pass through its gates are without any hope of future redemption or restoration. They are eternally condemned. This one truth is probably the one most repulsive to those who reject the biblical doctrine of hell. How can eternal punishment be just? Does not the punishment far exceed the crime?

When thinking about the eternal nature of hell, two truths must be considered: (1) We must take into account the abhorrent nature of sin. Sin committed against an infinitely worthy God is deserving of eternal punishment. To kick a dog is a terrible thing, but it is nothing compared to a man hitting his wife or slapping his king. How much greater is that crime which opposes an infinitely great and worthy God (Psalm 145:3)? (2) The punishment of hell is eternal, because throughout eternity the wicked continue in their rebellion without repentance. We must not assume that the wicked repent on the day of judgment or even after a short stay in hell. Rather their hatred of God, hardness of heart, and shameless rebellion continue throughout eternity. They were cast into hell as haters of God, and haters of God they remain. Eternal rebellion demands eternal punishment.

1. How is hell described in the following Scriptures? What do these descriptions communicate to us about the eternal nature of hell?

   a. E_____ F_____ *(Matthew 18:8; 25:41; Jude 7)*

   _____

   _____

   _____

   _____

   _____

   b. E_____ P_____ *(Matthew 25:46)*

   _____

   _____

   _____

   _____

   c. E_____ D_____ *(II Thessalonians 1:9):*

   _____

   _____

   _____

   _____

> **Note:** Although some would wrongly argue that the word *destruction* indicates a ceasing of existence, the word *eternal* makes this interpretation impossible. *In hell, the wicked are given over to an existence that can rightly be described as continual destruction.*

2. What do the following biblical texts teach us about the eternal nature of hell and the eternal punishment measured out upon the wicked?

   Mark 9:47-48

   _____

   _____

   _____

   _____

   Revelation 14:11

   _____

   _____

   _____

   _____

   Revelation 20:10; Matthew 25:41

   _____

   _____

   _____

   _____

3. Many who deny the eternal nature of hell would never deny the eternal nature of heaven. However, consistency requires that if one rejects the eternal nature of hell, he must also reject the eternal nature of heaven. How does **Matthew 25:46** demonstrate this truth?

   _____

   _____

   _____

   _____

   Note: It would be inconsistent to give two contradictory meanings to the same word in the same sentence. If "eternal" punishment does not really mean that the wicked are punished forever, then "eternal" life does not really mean that the righteous live forever in the presence of God.

A BIBLICAL DESCRIPTION OF HELL

In the Scriptures, many graphic and striking descriptions of hell are given. Whether they are to be taken as literal or not has been a long-standing debate even among conservative scholars. Is hell a place of literal fire and darkness, of brimstone and smoke? If someone denies a literal interpretation of these descriptions with the purpose of diminishing the sufferings of the wicked in hell, they are to be dismissed. However, it is acceptable to hold these descriptions to be figurative in the sense that they are an attempt to describe something so terrifying that it goes beyond the capacity of the human mind to conceive and beyond the power of our human language to communicate. To describe the terrors of hell, the biblical writers used the greatest terrors known to man on earth, but one can be assured that hell is worse than anything found on earth. Fire, darkness, brimstone (*i.e.* sulfur), and smoke are only a feeble attempt to describe a reality far more terrifying than even these words can convey. In the same way that the glories of heaven cannot be comprehended by the human mind or communicated through human language, the terrors of hell are beyond our comprehension and ability to describe.

1. How is hell described in the following Scriptures? What do these descriptions communicate to us about the nature of hell?

   a. *F_____ (Matthew 3:10; 7:19): Throughout the Scriptures, the idea of fire is used to communicate the judgment and wrath of God revealed against sin and the sinner. It is* God's holy and just reaction to all that contradicts His nature and will. It is fierce, terrifying, and irresistible. As *terrifying* and *intensely painful* as literal fire is to a burning man, it cannot begin to describe the fire of God's wrath that is measured out against the wicked in hell.

   b. *E_____ F_____ (Matthew 18:8; 25:41): The emphasis here is that the sufferings of the wicked in hell are forever.* There is no hope of redemption or restoration for those in hell.

   c. *U_____ F_____ (Matthew 3:12): The idea communicated here is that the torments of hell will not only be eternal, but undiminished.* There will never be any relief for the condemned.

d. *L_____ of F_____ and B_____ (**Revelation 20:10**): This description is given to communicate the immensity and power of hell.* It is not just a sprinkle or small stream of torment, but the inhabitants of hell will be like those lost at sea in a massive, churning ocean of God's wrath, battered and cast to and fro by the violent and never ending waves of God's righteous indignation, like men drowning in a massive, churning caldron of fire.

e. *F_____ of F_____ (**Matthew 13:42**): The truth communicated here is one of intensity.* In a furnace, all of the terrifying elements of fire are intensified—there is little chance for the heat to escape, no rain to dampen the flames, and no breeze to bring refreshment or relief. The intensity of hell's sufferings will never be diminished.

f. *O_____ D_____ (**Matthew 8:12; 22:13; 25:30**): The truth communicated here is one of alienation.* The inhabitants of hell are cast out and no place is found for them. They are not only alienated from God, but from fellowship with others. It is a place of absolute and unbearable isolation, apart from the life and light of God.

g. *B_____ D_____ (**Jude 13**): There are very few things more solitary or more incarcerating than pitch-black darkness.* There is the greatest sense of doom or hopelessness related to such darkness.

h. *S_____ D_____ (**Revelation 20:14; 21:8**): The final destiny of the wicked is the very opposite of the believer.* There is no longer a fear of death for the believer (Hebrews 2:15) because death is no more (Revelation 21:4). In contrast, the wicked will live in a state of never-ending death. They will have a conscious existence, but with none of the blessings, hopes, or joys of life.

2. Having considered some of the descriptive names of hell, write your thoughts. How would you describe hell to another?

_____

_____

_____

_____

WARNINGS TO AVOID HELL AT ANY COST

The terrors of hell are clearly communicated in the scriptural warnings to avoid hell at any cost. Of all the terrors that could ever come upon a man, hell is the worst. It is important to note that Jesus Christ spoke about hell more than all the other biblical writers combined. He clearly and unapologetically taught about the realities of hell and gave men the greatest warnings to flee from the wrath to come. The texts below are two of the gravest warnings giving by Jesus Christ concerning the terrors of hell. Write your thoughts. What do these warnings communicate to us about the terrors of hell and the need to fear it?

Matthew 10:28

Luke 12:5

3. Jesus and the biblical writers not only taught about the terrors of hell, but they warned men to avoid the condemnation of hell at any cost. What do the following Scriptures teach us regarding this truth?

Luke 13:24

Note: The word *strive* comes from a Greek word meaning *contend*, *struggle*, *labor fervently*, or *labor with tremendous zeal*.

Matthew 18:8-9; Mark 9:43-48

_____

_____

_____

_____

Note: These passages are not to be taken literally—Jesus is not teaching the virtues of self-mutilation as a means of restraining our sinful passions. He is simply teaching that we must deal radically with sin because of its terrifying consequences. A man who deals with sin in a trifling way will never escape the fire of hell.

MAN'S ONLY HOPE

Having come to the end of our study about man, we have reached some very solemn conclusions. The sin of Adam has reached the entire human race. Every man is a morally corrupt being, hostile toward God, and unwilling to submit to His will. All are capable of unspeakable sins and perversions, and all are therefore worthy of the just condemnation of a holy and righteous God. The Scripture is clear—all men without exception stand condemned before God without excuse or alibi, and man can do nothing to change his circumstances or reconcile himself to God. This is a dreadful truth, but it must be believed and accepted if we are to comprehend the great salvation which God accomplished for His people through Jesus Christ.

The following Scriptures are a fitting conclusion for this study because they not only declare the solemn truth about our inability to save ourselves, but they also proclaim the great hope of salvation through the mercy of God revealed in Jesus Christ. Consider each Scripture, writing out both the *solemn truth* and the *great hope* that is found in each.

Psalm 130:3-4:

a. *The Solemn Truth (v. 3):*

b. *The Great Hope (v. 4):*

Romans 3:19-26:

a. *The Solemn Truth (vs. 19-20):*

b. *The Great Hope (vs. 21-26):*

Romans 7:24-8:2:

a. *The Solemn Truth (7:24):*

b. *The Great Hope (7:25-8:2):*

_____

_____

_____

_____

Galatians 3:22:

a. *The Solemn Truth:*

_____

_____

_____

_____

b. *The Great Hope:*

_____

_____

_____

_____

The truth about man is devastating to anyone whose conscience has been awakened by the Holy Spirit. As the apostle Paul cried out, "Wretched man that I am! Who will set me free from the body of this death?" (Romans 7:24). The answer to Paul's question and the solution to man's dreadful predicament is found in Christ alone—the Gospel, or Good News of His saving work on our behalf.

The Psalmist tells us that if the Lord should keep a record of our trespasses against Him, there would not be a single man on earth who could stand before Him in judgment (Psalm 130:3-4). Our iniquities have gone over our heads and as a heavy burden their weight is too much for us to bear (Psalm 38:4). Sin is mankind's greatest problem and the singular source of all the maladies that ruin us as individuals and as collective societies. Therefore our two greatest needs are salvation from the condemnation of sin, and deliverance from its power. Both of which are provided for in the person of Jesus Christ and in His saving work on our behalf.

The Bible declares unequivocally that God is compassionate and gracious, slow to anger, and abounding in lovingkindess (Exodus 34:6-8). Therefore, He does not take delight in the death of the wicked, but rather that he should turn from his way and live (Ezekiel 18:23). Regardless of the depth of a man's sin or the extent of his rebellion, he is offered both pardon and cleansing if he will forsake his way and return to the Lord. The Psalmist even goes so far as to say that God will forgive his lawless deeds, cover his sins, and no longer take his trespasses into account (Psalm 32:1-2; Romans 4:6-8).

This is astounding news, but it does present us with something of theological or philosophical dilemma: How can a good and righteous God grant pardon to wicked men? Shall not the judge of all the earth do right (Genesis 18:25)? Can a just God be apathetic toward sin or brush it under the rug as though it never happened? Can a holy God bring wicked men into fellowship with Himself and still be holy? The Scriptures themselves declare that, "He who justifies the wicked… is an abomination to the LORD" (Proverbs 17:15). How then can God forgive the wicked without compromising His own character? Again, the answer is found in the person and work of Christ.

According to the Scriptures, man has sinned and the wages of sin is death (Romans 3:23; 6:23). God is just and the demands of His law must be satisfied before the guilty can be pardoned (Proverbs 17:15). In the fullness of time, the Son of God became a man and walked on this earth in perfect obedience to the law of God (Galatians 4:4). At the end of His life and according to the will of the Father, He was crucified by the hands of wicked men (Acts 2:23). On the cross, He stood in the place of His guilty people and their sin was imputed to Him (II Corinthians 5:21). As the sin bearer, He became accursed of God, forsaken of God, and crushed under the weight of God's wrath (Galatians 3:13; Matthew 27:46; Isaiah 53:10). Through His death, the debt for sin was paid, the demands of God's justice were satisfied, and the wrath of God was appeased. In this manner, God solved the great dilemma. He has justly punished the sins of His people in the death of His only Son, and therefore, may freely justify all who place their hope in Him.

Through the death of His Son, God may now be both just and the justifier of even the most vile sinner who places his trust in Him (Romans 3:26). However, the Gospel is more than liberation from the condemnation of sin; it is also deliverance from sin's power. In his first epistle, the apostle John tells us, "Whoever believes that Jesus is the Christ has been born of God" (I John 5:1). This new birth which enables a man to repent and believe unto salvation, also enables him to walk in newness of life (Romans 6:4). Through the regenerating work of the Holy Spirit, the believer's heart of stone, which was spiritually dead and unresponsive to God, has been replaced with a heart of living flesh that is both willing and able to hear His voice and follow Him (Ezekiel 36:25-27). Though he was once a bad tree bearing bad fruit, he is now a good tree planted by streams of water, yielding fruit in its season, and with leaves that do not wither (Matthew 7:17-18; Psalm 1:3). Thus the believer is not only justified, but is also the very workmanship of God created in Christ Jesus for good works (Ephesians 2:10). In fact, this ongoing moral transformation in the believer's life is the basis of his assurance and the evidence of true conversion.

As we have said from the beginning, the Gospel is astounding news, but the question remains: "How may it be obtained?" "What must a man do to be saved?" The answer is clear, he must "repent and believe the Gospel" (Mark 1:15). The many Scriptures in this workbook have already refuted any argument or suggestion that a man might be saved by his own virtue and merit. In ourselves, we are destitute of both, and even what may be called righteous deeds before other men, are nothing but filthy rags before God (Isaiah 64:6). Therefore to be saved, to obtain the salvation promised in the Gospel, we must reject any and all confidence in the flesh, and trust in Christ alone (Philippians 3:3). The Christian is the man who has agreed with God concerning his sinful state, has renounced all confidence in his own virtue and merit, and has place all his hope for salvation in the person and work of Jesus Christ.

For God so loved the world, that He gave His only begotten Son, that
whoever believes in Him shall not perish, but have eternal life.
- John 3:16

ABOUT THE AUTHOR

Paul Washer became a believer while attending the University of Texas studying to become an oil and gas lawyer. He completed his undergraduate studies and enrolled at Southwestern Theological Seminary where he received his Master of Divinity degree. Paul left the states shortly after graduation as a North American missionary to Peru.

Paul ministered as a missionary in Peru for 10 years, during which time he founded the HeartCry Missionary Society to support Peruvian Church planters. HeartCry's work now supports over 100 indigenous missionaries in 20 different countries throughout Eastern Europe, South America, Africa, Asia, and the Middle East.

An itinerant preacher, Paul also frequently teaches at his home church. At present, Paul serves as the Director of HeartCry Missionary Society and resides in Radford, Virginia with his wife Charo and two sons Ian and Evan, and one daughter Rowan.

ABOUT HEARTCRY MISSIONARY SOCIETY

As Christians, we are called, commissioned, and commanded to lay down our lives so that the Gospel might be preached to every creature under heaven. Second only to loving God, this is to be our magnificent obsession. There is no nobler task for which we may give our lives than promoting the glory of God in the redemption of men through the preaching of the Gospel of Jesus Christ. If the Christian is truly obedient to the Great Commission, he will give his life either to go down into the well or to hold the rope for those who go down. Either way, the same radical commitment is required.

The Christian who is truly passionate about the glory of God and confident in His sovereignty will not be unmoved by the billions of people in the world who have yet to hear the Gospel of Jesus Christ. If we are truly Christlike, the lost multitude of humanity will move us to compassion (Matthew 9:36), even to great sorrow and unceasing grief (Romans 9:2). The sincerity of our Christian confession should be questioned if we are not willing to do all within our means to make Christ known among the nations and to endure all things for the sake of God's elect (II Timothy 2:10).

While we recognize that the needs of mankind are many and his sufferings are diverse, we believe that they all spring from a common origin—the radical depravity of his heart, his enmity toward God, and his rejection of truth. Therefore, we believe that the greatest benefit to mankind can be accomplished through the preaching of the Gospel and the establishment of local churches that proclaim the full counsel of God's Word and minister according to its commands, precepts, and wisdom. Such a work cannot be accomplished through the arm of the flesh, but only through the supernatural providence of God and the means which He has ordained: biblical preaching, intercessory prayer, sacrificial service, unconditional love, and true Christlikeness.

OUR PURPOSE

The chief end of all mission work is the Glory of God. Our greatest concern is that His Name be great among the nations, from the rising to the setting of the sun (Malachi 1:11), and that the Lamb who was slain might receive the full reward for His sufferings (Revelation 7:9-10). We find our great purpose and motivation not in man or his needs, but in God, His commitment to His own glory, and our God-given desire to see Him worshipped in every nation, tribe, people, and language. We find our great confidence not in the Church's ability to fulfill the Great Commission, but in God's unlimited and unhindered power to accomplish all He has decreed.

OUR MISSION

The goal of our ministry is to glorify God through the preaching of the Gospel and the establishment of biblical churches throughout the world.

Reasons:
- A biblical church is the will of God. The establishment of local churches was the goal of apostolic ministry (Ephesians 3:10-11, 21; 4:11-13).
- A biblical church is the result or 'mature fruit' of a genuine work of God. Therefore, the goal of planting a biblical church will be the means of guiding and validating all our missionary efforts.
- A biblical church is the *"pillar and support"* of truth. Therefore, it is the great and enduring bulwark against error (I Timothy 3:15). The church is the *"salt of the earth,"* and the only entity that can preserve a nation or people from self-deceit and self-deception.

- A biblical church is the only means of creating a self-sustaining, ever-multiplying mission effort.

Nature of the New Testament Church:

- It is local and visible.

- It is spiritual and organic. It is more an organism than an organization, institution, or mechanism.

- It is autonomous—the fellowship is self-governing and self-supporting.

- It is collective or communal. Its members are interdependent, ministering to one another according to their callings and giftings.

- It is doctrinally or theologically driven (vs. pragmatism and cultural sensitivity).

- It is missionary—the fellowship is directly involved in the establishment of new churches of like faith and practice.

- Its chief end and motivation is the glory of God in Christ.

ESSENTIAL CONVICTIONS OF HeartCry MISSIONARY SOCIETY

1. **Missions is an Impossibility apart from the Power of God.** All men of every culture are born radically depraved, at enmity with God, and restraining the truth. The conversion of a man and the advancement of missions are an absolute impossibility apart from the supernatural power of the Holy Spirit in regeneration. Modern church growth strategies and many new mission methodologies often overlook this essential truth.

2. **A True Gospel must be Proclaimed.** The Gospel is the power of God for salvation (Romans 1:16) and the preaching of the Gospel is the great *means* and *methodology* of missions. The Gospel is, first and foremost, God in Christ reconciling the world to Himself (II Corinthians 5:19). It answers the eternal question of how a just God can rightly justify wicked men (Romans 3:26). It points to Christ alone, who bore the sins of His people upon the cross, was forsaken of God, and crushed under the full force of His just wrath against sin. The Good News of the Gospel is that through Christ's death, the justice of God was satisfied, and salvation was won for a great multitude of people. This is evidenced by the resurrection of Jesus Christ from the dead—*"He who was delivered over because of our transgressions, and was raised because of our justification"* (Romans 4:25).

3. **The Gospel Transcends Culture.** The greatest need of all men of every culture is the clear proclamation of the Gospel. Men are saved through the Gospel and continue in sanctification through continued growth in the full counsel of God's Word. Although differences in culture are to be considered, it is more important for the missionary to be biblically sensitive than culturally sensitive. A missionary was once asked how he preached the Gospel to a certain remote tribe. He declared, "I do not preach the Gospel to a remote tribe. I preach the Gospel to men!"

4. **Incarnational Missions is Essential.** Although there may be some effective non-personal means of communicating the Gospel, there is no substitute for one man living among a people, teaching the Gospel to them, and living out his faith before them. God sent His own Son, and He became flesh and dwelt among us (John 1:1,14; 3:16).

5. **Superficial Evangelism is one of the Great Obstacles to Missions.** Non-theological preaching, entertaining skits, and Gospel films are no substitute for the biblical exposition of the Gospel. Inviting men to raise their hands and pray a prayer is no substitute for the biblical call to repentance, faith, and personal discipleship. Biblical assurance of salvation does not flow from a past decision or a prayer, but from the examination of one's enduring lifestyle in the light of Scripture.

6. **Church Planting is the Primary Work of Missions.** There are many gifts and callings in the body of Christ, but on all of them are to work together on the mission field with the primary goal of planting a biblical church. It is one thing to do mass evangelism and to boast of the numbers of decisions; it is quite another to establish a biblical church.

7. **True Missions is Costly.** Amy Carmichael explained that missions is no more and no less than an opportunity to die. We live in a fallen world that is at enmity with God and opposes His truth; therefore, missions and suffering go hand in hand. Any advancement of the kingdom of Christ into the dominion of the devil will be met with warfare. There are many countries and people groups where martyrdom cannot be avoided.

www.HeartCryMissionary.Com

OTHER TITLES AVAILABLE FROM

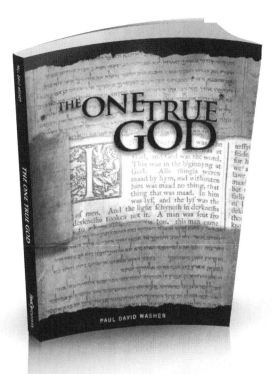

The One True God, a Biblical study of the Doctrine of God - by Paul Washer
Workbook: 8.5" x 11" (21.59 x 27.94 cm)
Page Count: 192
ISBN: 1466316306

A unique kind of workbook, *The One True God* intends not just to teach truth but to lead to an encounter with the living God. Beneath that goal the book aims to ground believers in orthodox Christian theology and the actual contents of the Bible. Students are encouraged to thoughtfully draw conclusions from the *Scriptures* rather than to merely absorb the principles, inferences, and illustrations set before them by the *author*. For this reason the book does not include such material and instead focuses on digesting the Scriptures directly.

> "Paul David Washer's study guide on the doctrine of God, *The One True God*, is the best introductory work known to me. It sets out great truths in clear and balanced form. Human authorities are not quoted but it is evident that the author is familiar with the literature of historic Christianity and accordingly he misses the pitfalls into which others might fall. Young Christians could scarcely spend their time better than working carefully through these pages."

– IAIN H. MURRAY
CO-FOUNDER AND EDITORIAL DIRECTOR
FOR THE BANNER OF TRUTH TRUST

Made in the USA
Charleston, SC
04 October 2012